Praise for
Cast-Iron Cooking for Two

"If you've ever longingly eyed a recipe but had to pass it up because it served a small army or used a small army's kitchen's worth of pans, bow down to Joanna Pruess. She has created a book of delicious, just-right-for-two dishes that use basically one pan. Your copy will be dog-eared in no time."

—David Leite, publisher of the James Beard Award-winning website Leite's Culinaria (LCcooks.com)

"Joanna Pruess's *Cast-Iron Cooking for Two* is a magical work. With her easy, accessible, and delicious recipes for two, Joanna encourages cooks to share the magic that is cast-iron cooking at its best, even for small gatherings."

—Mark Kelly, public relations manager, Lodge Cast Iron

"A lovely book and full of wonderful ideas. I can think of dedicated cooks wanting to try one a week, if not more often. I'm cooking my way through the book."

—Nancy Harmon Jenkins, author of *The Four Seasons of Pasta*

Cast-Iron
COOKING for TWO

75 QUICK AND EASY SKILLET RECIPES

JOANNA PRUESS

PHOTOGRAPHS BY NOAH FECKS
FOREWORD BY MARK KELLY

Skyhorse Publishing

For Nicole, Ben, and Justin Pruess, Lindsey Sterling Pruess, and my grandsons Jackson and Levi, you enrich my life beyond measure. Without your love and support, life would be as boring as unseasoned, cold mashed potatoes.

Skyhorse Publishing books may be purchased in bulk at special discounts for sales promotion, corporate gifts, fund-raising, or educational purposes. Special editions can also be created to specifications. For details, contact the Special Sales Department, Skyhorse Publishing, 307 West 36th Street, 11th Floor, New York, NY 10018 or info@skyhorsepublishing.com.

Skyhorse® and Skyhorse Publishing® are registered trademarks of Skyhorse Publishing, Inc.®, a Delaware corporation.

Visit our website at www.skyhorsepublishing.com.

10 9 8 7 6 5 4 3 2 1

Library of Congress Cataloging-in-Publication Data is available on file.

Cover design by Laura Klynstra
Cover photo credit: Noah Fecks

Print ISBN: 978-1-5107-4803-3
Ebook ISBN: 978-1-5107-4804-0

Printed in China

Contents

Asian Salade Niçoise with Sesame-Crusted Tuna, page 121

Foreword

WELCOME TO MS. WIZARD'S KITCHEN

For decades, young TV viewers were captivated by the antics of Don Herbert, the host of *Mr. Wizard*, as he used household items to teach the basics of chemistry and physics. His successful experiments enhanced the prevailing attitude that all things were possible through science.

Turning the clock forward, Joanna Pruess's inspiring new cookbook, *Cast-Iron Cooking for Two*, ably demonstrates Mr. Wizard's theme that endless magic is possible by using of what lies around your house, especially in the kitchen.

Indeed, there isn't a better category of cookware than cast iron to represent culinary science and the food history of many families. The same pots and pans that nurtured bygone generations are invaluable for today's home cooks, many of whom—as couples, two friends, or a pair of family members—crave tasty and easy-to-prepare meals. Appropriately, all the recipes in *Cast-Iron Cooking for Two,* from traditional favorites to stylish contemporary dishes, use a 6-, 8-, or 10-inch skillet, grill pan, or griddle.

The cookware's versatility is legendary. Anyone can sear a steak, bake Aunt Mary's cobbler, braise Grandma's short ribs, sauté fish fillets, or resurrect the family's deep-fried chicken recipe in cast iron. The pans also shine with contemporary favorites like stir-fried vegetables and baked flatbreads, plus a skillet of meat or vegetables that can be slid under the broiler with results that always exceed expectations.

As much as American cooks maintain a sense of ownership to cast iron's legacy and lore, Joanna's wide-ranging but well-curated collection of recipes reflects the universal diversity of food cultures that use cast-iron pans. While some include ingredients that may cause readers to flip the pages in search of dishes with more familiar spices, fear not. With a little planning, any ingredient used in *Cast-Iron Cooking for Two* is readily available online and can be shipped to your location as quickly as novels, electronics, and exercise equipment from other websites.

Just where did cast iron come from? Historically, pig iron and steel were melted at high temperatures and poured into sand-cast molds to create durable and versatile cookware—an age-old practice. So why are the pans suddenly popping up on store shelves now? In reality, cast iron has been enjoying a renaissance for almost two decades.

Much of the category's growth can be traced to Lodge Cast Iron's introduction of foundry-seasoned cast-iron items in 2002. The resurgence also received an assist from television cooking shows, food and lifestyle magazines, and cookbooks featuring recipes prepared in cast-iron cookware.

Since 2002, cast-iron cookware, including enamel-coated pans, has been the fastest growing sector of the cookware market, rising from 4 percent of US sales to 15 percent in 2018. Sales throughout Europe, Scandinavia, Asia, Australia, and New Zealand continue to enjoy positive results, as well.

The pans' humble origins are still cherished by owners who revere the cooking performance of their pieces and relish passing their passion onto the next generation.

Joanna Pruess's *Cast-Iron Cooking for Two* is a magical work. With her easy, accessible, and delicious recipes for two, Joanna encourages cooks to share the magic that is cast-iron cooking at its best, even for small gatherings.

—Mark H. Kelly
Public Relations Manager,
Lodge Cast Iron,
South Pittsburg, Tennessee

Introduction

CAST-IRON COOKING FOR TWO: WHY IT WORKS FOR ME TODAY

When I started cooking in college, I discovered that foods cooked in cast-iron pans had a certain cachet that definitely helped my social life. Guys thought steaks charred in black skillets were sexy and macho, as well as delicious. Mom's creamy mac 'n' cheese (made in her Dutch oven) was a terrific icebreaker at an open house, and there was never a bite left of my seasonal cobblers under crisp streusel topping. I soon realized sharing food was my destiny and cast iron played an important supporting role.

In the ensuing decades, I've entertained my family, friends, and clients with meals ranging from homey to lavish—all cooked in cast iron. Over the years, my adventures throughout Europe, climbing the Great Wall of China near Beijing and the Pyramid of the Magician in Mexico's Yucatán, the Middle East, and India introduced me to unique flavors and cooking techniques that were adaptable to cast iron. Along the way, I've written books and articles about the cookware's durability and versatility and

watched as restaurants started serving both comfort food and modern dishes directly from the pan. I continue to entertain and cook for others, but these days it's usually me plus one, an intimacy that is both rewarding and fun after years of feeding many people at once.

If my 14-inch cast-iron skillet and large Dutch oven mostly stay on a shelf, my 6-, 8-, and 10-inch skillets are ever-present on the stove, as they're the pans I reach for first. They are also the ones I use most often in *Cast-Iron Cooking for Two,* which combines two passions. The first is the new stage in my culinary journey, cooking for two. The second is my ongoing enthusiasm for the simple versatility of cast-iron cooking, starting with the comfort food of my college days on through my more recent exploration with how cast iron is utilized in cultures throughout the world in both simple and complex dishes.

I suggest that this book is for anyone who enjoys preparing and eating delicious food as well as the adventure of discovering new and exciting dishes from across the street and around the world. I love how unique tastes, textures, colors, smells, and even sounds can be woven into the simplest dishes to make them seem new. Along the way, my discoveries introduced me to exotic ingredients and unfamiliar techniques. In sharing them with you, I hope you'll find these recipes both appealing and approachable.

In *Cast-Iron Cooking for Two*, there are more than seventy-five just-for-two recipes that are made in cast-iron pans, from the cute little 6-inch skillet to the 8- and 10-inch versions, as well as a grill pan and griddle. These include homey favorites like Mom's Mac 'n' Cheese with Bacon (page 44) and Blackberry-Candied Ginger Crisp (page 193), along with dishes inspired by my global adventures, the discovery of unique food products, and old and new friends. You won't have to leave your kitchen to enjoy the flavors of Morocco in *Goryba*: Moroccan Orange-Sesame Shortbread (page 201) from a creative chef in Fez; in Pan-Fried Catfish Kerala-Style with Indian Tartar Sauce (page 106) you'll taste bright Southern Indian flavors from that tropical region I fell in love with; and you might be as surprised and pleased as I was by the combination of Frozen Cranberries with Hot Caramel Sauce and Rye-Almond Spice Cookies: A Finnish Dessert (page 198), as served to me on a midsummer's day in Helsinki.

At home, a party of two has many advantages and very few rules. What and when you eat, for example, can change on a whim. While the chapters in this book are organized traditionally, from breakfast through desserts, the recipes aren't necessarily fixed to a time of day—just as many of us eat today. Buckwheat Crepes with Smoked Salmon (page 16) in the breakfast and lunch chapter can be served for lunch, and even dinner. Blueberry-Lemon Clafouti (page 195) makes a celebratory breakfast in addition to dessert after dinner. And side dishes like Roasted Corn Pancakes with Cherry Tomato Salsa and Goat Cheese (page 71) or Sweet Potato Pancakes with Asian Brussels Sprouts Slaw (page 80) can be an ideal lunch, the center of a light dinner, or midmorning or late afternoon fare for anyone with an irregular schedule.

Breaking the rules is fun! Imagine devouring warm Ooey-Gooey Coffee-Toffee Chocolate Brownies (page 207) straight from a 6-inch skillet. With ice cream on top, you'll just need two spoons to literally dig in. Call it lunch or dessert or just pure decadence.

When I first downsized my cooking, rethinking grocery shopping and cooking for smaller meals took thought and practice, much of which I gleaned while writing *Soup for Two* a couple of years ago. Be assured, I still love to create and eat delicious foods, but I also like to guard my energy and time. So I've included some of my findings in the shopping suggestions on pages 216 to 219. and sprinkled other tips throughout the book. Throughout the recipes, you'll also learn about gadgets and equipment I found helpful, tips for measuring smaller amounts, and shortcuts that won't shortchange the results. For example, using high-quality pesto, the best purchased puff pastry or pizza dough, and flash-frozen sliced peaches harvested at the peak of ripeness can save you time and hassles.

Whenever I use a unique product in the recipes, I mention the brand name, signaling a company as one I trust. Along with Internet suppliers, supermarkets and specialty food shops have risen to the challenge of providing small packages of broth, precut vegetables, spice mixtures, etc., and I give suggestions for using these in the Appendices. There are also guidelines there for what you can cook in cast iron (almost everything) and a couple of things to avoid, as well as the best methods of cleaning your pots and pans.

Dining for two has shown me that sharing homemade food with a friend, partner, child, or grandchild does more than nourish the body; it can spark a conversation that lifts the spirits or be a calming oasis in our stressful world. What or where you eat—a snack at a kitchen counter or whole meal at a fully set dining table—isn't important. Even with prep and cleanup, cooking at home often turns out to be more satisfying than restaurant meals. It's a communion.

The book's cast-iron recipes range from the Homey Oven-Roasted Chicken Thighs and Legs with Pan Gravy (page 141) on the cover, to Chipotle-Cinnamon Molten Lava Cake, the last recipe on page 202. I hope you'll find among them many dishes perfect for any occasion when it's just the two of you. That said, only you can determine the size of your hunger. If you have smaller appetites, why not invite another guest? In the end, I think food is best when shared.

Finally, speaking about sharing, nothing in this book is etched in stone. I've offered my ideas, but hope you will feel free to make these dishes your own. Change the spices, add a different vegetable, or substitute chicken for fish. If this book inspires you to prepare and share meals, I'll be delighted.

Happy cooking and eating,

—Joanna Pruess
New York, NY

1. Breakfast & Lunch

SHAKSHUKA

This dish of poached eggs in spiced tomato sauce is said to have originated in Tunisia, where the word shakshuka *means a "mixture" in Arabic slang. Its fame spread throughout the Middle East, and recently the dish has become popular in the United States. Enjoy it as a bright, appealing entrée at any time of the day. The tomato sauce includes sautéed onion and an Anaheim chile or a bell pepper, if you prefer less heat.*

Add the tomato paste if the tomatoes taste slightly acidic. Pita bread triangles are essential for dipping in the sauce and runny eggs. Cheese on top is a matter of choice.

1½ tablespoons extra-virgin olive oil
1 large Anaheim chile, seeds and membranes removed, finely chopped (½–¾ cup)
1 small onion, chopped
2 large cloves garlic, finely chopped
1 teaspoon ground cumin
1 teaspoon smoked paprika
1 (14.5-ounce) can fire roasted and diced tomatoes, undrained
½ cup water
1 teaspoon tomato paste, if needed
Kosher salt or coarse sea salt
3–4 large eggs
2 tablespoons chopped flat-leaf parsley or mint
2 tablespoons crumbled feta cheese
Warm pita, cut into triangles, to serve

Heat an 8-inch cast-iron skillet over medium-high heat until hot but not smoking. Add the olive oil, Anaheim chile, and onion and sauté until soft and golden, 6 to 7 minutes, stirring often. Add the garlic, cumin, and paprika and cook for 30 seconds.

Stir in the tomatoes and water, adjust the heat so the liquid is simmering, and cook for 15 minutes. Add the optional tomato paste, if desired. Season to taste with salt.

Reduce the heat to low. Crack one egg into a glass or measuring cup. Using a wooden spoon, make a well in the tomato sauce. Holding the space with the spoon, pour in the egg. Repeat with the remaining eggs, spacing the indentations evenly in the pan. Cover and cook until the yolks are just set, about 6 minutes or longer, occasionally spooning the tomato mixture over the whites but not disturbing the yolks.

Sprinkle the parsley and cheese over the dish and serve with pita bread triangles.

SAVORY DUTCH BABY WITH SAUTÉED VEGETABLES AND PESTO

For years, I baked puffy, Yorkshire pudding-like apple pancakes for dessert or brunch. My kids and I called them German pancakes, or pfannkuchen, *and they were always wide-eyed as the risen pancake came out of the oven, even though they knew they quickly deflated. Recently, I learned they were called Dutch babies because someone somewhere confused "Deutsch" and "Dutch."*

These days, savory versions have become increasingly popular. In this one, the batter includes a little Parmigiano-Reggiano, and sautéed zucchini, peppers, and onion combined with a little pesto are spooned on top. It's a tasty brunch or lunch choice. Many vegetables can be substituted. If using purchased pesto, be sure to check the ingredients for additives and taste it before adding it to a recipe.

1 tablespoon Quick Homemade Pesto (page 12) or high-quality purchased pesto
1 tablespoon extra-virgin olive oil
½ cup diced onion
½ cup diced red bell pepper
½ cup zucchini, quartered lengthwise and thinly sliced
1 large clove garlic, finely chopped garlic
¼ teaspoon dried thyme leaves
Kosher salt or sea salt
Freshly ground black pepper
2 large eggs
⅓ cup all-purpose flour
⅓ cup milk
3 tablespoons grated Parmigiano-Reggiano
1 tablespoon melted unsalted butter, plus 1 tablespoon for the pan
2 teaspoons minced flat-leaf parsley

Make the Quick Homemade Pesto.

In a medium-sized skillet, heat the oil over medium-high heat until hot but not smoking. Add the onion, pepper, and zucchini and sauté until wilted and lightly colored, about 3 to 4 minutes. Stir in the garlic and thyme and cook for 30 seconds. Let the vegetables cool slightly, then stir in the pesto, season to taste with salt and pepper, and set aside.

Position an oven rack with enough space for the pancake to rise above the skillet's edge. Place an 8-inch cast-iron skillet in the oven and preheat to 425°F.

In an electric blender or mini-processor, combine the eggs, flour, milk, Parmigiano-Reggiano, melted butter, parsley, and a pinch of salt. Process until completely smooth.

(Directions continued on next page)

Carefully remove the skillet from the oven, add the remaining butter, swirl to cover the bottom of the pan, and immediately pour in the batter. Return the pan to the oven and bake until the sides have risen, the edges are browned, and the pancake has begun to puff up in the center, 7 to 8 minutes. Remove from the oven, spoon the vegetables in the middle, and serve.

QUICK HOMEMADE PESTO

Makes ½ cup

In my enthusiasm for basil, sometimes I end up with too much. Short of tossing it out, a couple of my favorite "saves" are as a small batch of pesto (which always gets used quickly in my house) or basil oil (page 63) to drizzle on salads, grilled fish, or vegetables. Do not use the stems or damaged leaves.

1 cup packed fresh basil leaves or mixed with flat-leaf parsley
1 clove garlic
2 tablespoons pine nuts
⅓ cup extra-virgin olive oil
¼ cup freshly grated Parmigiano-Reggiano or Pecorino Romano cheese
Kosher salt and freshly ground black pepper, to taste

In a mini food processor, combine the basil and parsley, if using, with the garlic and pine nuts and pulse until coarsely chopped. Add the oil and process until chunky smooth. Add the cheese and pulse until almost smooth. Season with salt and pepper to taste. If not using right away, scrape into a resealable jar, refrigerate, and use within a few weeks.

CRUNCHY POTATO LATKES WITH BACON AND EGGS

Crispy potato pancakes or latkes are among my favorite indulgences. Eating two, however, pushes the limit, so these are just slightly larger than one serving, so you won't feel guilty. Combine them with bacon—another favorite of mine—and eggs for a scrumptious brunch or light supper. If you like, blend the bacon fat left in the skillet with vegetable oil and use it to fry the latkes.

To ensure crunchy pancakes, squeeze as much liquid as you can from the potatoes. Once in the pan, don't flatten them with a spatula as they'll become dense and you'll lose those tasty wisps of potato. To check the seasonings ahead of time, fry a tiny disk of the mixture in hot oil until golden and taste.

These latkes are also delicious when paired with smoked salmon, crème fraîche, chopped red onions, and capers.

4 slices thick-cut bacon
1 medium-large baking potato
    (about 8 ounces), scrubbed
½ small onion, grated
2–3 tablespoons panko
¼ teaspoon kosher salt or sea salt
Freshly ground black pepper
3–5 large eggs
Canola or other vegetable oil plus
    bacon fat, if using, to measure
    ¼ inch
1 tablespoon unsalted butter
2–4 large eggs
Salt and pepper

Turn the oven or toaster oven to warm. Starting with a cold 10-inch cast-iron skillet, cook the bacon on top of the stove over medium-high heat until crisp, turning a few times. Remove, blot on paper towels, and keep warm in the oven. Leave the bacon fat in the skillet, if you will use it. Otherwise, wipe out the pan.

Using a box grater or food processor with a grating disk, shred the potato and put in a bowl. Grate the onion and add it to the potato. Using a clean towel, squeeze as much liquid as you can from the mixture and return it to a bowl. In a small bowl, beat one of the eggs. Stir in 2 tablespoons of the panko, salt, and pepper, and then combine with the potato-onion mixture, turning to blend evenly, adding more panko if the mixture is too wet.

Add enough oil to the bacon fat to measure about ½ inch deep and set over medium-high heat until

(Directions continued on next page)

hot but not smoking. Scoop up the potato mixture and gently form into two patties, about 3 inches in diameter, and carefully slide into the hot oil. Turn the heat down to medium and cook until the latkes are golden brown, 5 to 6 minutes. Do not press to compress. Turn and cook the second side until golden brown. Remove with a spatula and blot on paper towels. Serve with the bacon and eggs.

Wipe out the skillet, melt the butter, and scramble or fry the remaining eggs according to preference. Season to taste with salt and pepper. Serve one or two eggs per person along with one pancake and two slices of bacon.

BUCKWHEAT CREPES WITH SMOKED SALMON

Breizh Café is a wildly popular crêperie in Paris's Marais district that serves savory buckwheat and whole wheat crepes with several fillings all day long. Whether for brunch or even a light supper, I think you'll enjoy these earthy-tasting, dark buckwheat crepes with smoked salmon, crème fraîche, capers, red onions, and a squeeze of fresh lemon juice inspired by their menu. It's a satisfying and luxurious partnership.

I added a little all-purpose flour to the batter to keep the crepes pliable and thin enough to wrap around the salmon. A splash of sparkling water added at the end makes the batter lighter. Crepes are easy to make in a 10-inch round griddle pan, but a skillet about that size also works.

CREPES
- ¼ cup buckwheat flour (I use Bob's Red Mill whole grain)
- 2 tablespoons all-purpose flour
- ⅛ teaspoon sea salt
- ¼ cup whole milk
- 3 tablespoons water
- 1 large egg
- 1 tablespoon canola or other vegetable oil, plus oil to brush the pan
- 1 tablespoon sparkling water, or more if needed

FILLING
- 4 ounces thinly sliced smoked salmon
- 2 tablespoons crème fraîche or sour cream
- 1 tablespoon small capers
- 2 tablespoons finely chopped red onion
- 2–4 thin slices lemon
- Finely chopped dill, for garnish

In a bowl, combine the flour and salt. In a small measuring cup or bowl, whisk together the milk, water, egg, and oil until blended. Pour into the dry ingredients and whisk to completely blend. Cover and refrigerate for at least 2 hours or overnight.

Remove the batter from the refrigerator, and whisk in 1 tablespoon of sparkling water. The consistency should be that of thin cream. Add a little more water, if needed.

Heat a 10-inch cast-iron griddle or skillet over medium heat. Brush lightly with oil. When a few drops of water skitter across the surface, pour about ⅓ cup of the batter into the center of the pan, quickly rotate, and tip the pan to cover the whole surface, adding a few drops of batter, as needed, to cover any holes.

Cook until little bubbles form on the surface and it appears dull, about 1 minute. Using an offset or silicone spatula, lift the crepe with your fingers, and quickly turn it over. Cook the second side until lightly browned, about 1 minute more.

Remove to a plate and continue with the second crepe. If not using right away, cover with waxed paper and wrap tightly.

To serve: on each of two plates, lay a crepe with the nicest side down. Place the salmon on one side, fold the crepe into quarters, drizzle with crème fraîche, and add capers, red onion, and a squeeze of fresh lemon juice. Garnish with dill and serve.

PUMPKIN-CORNMEAL-CRANBERRY PANCAKES WITH CANDIED PECANS

These pancakes remind me of the tastes of Thanksgiving and Christmas rolled into one. Pumpkin, cornmeal, and dried cranberries, along with the flavors of pumpkin pie (easily bought already mixed in a single jar if your cupboard space is limited), are set off by candied pecans or pumpkin seeds and warm maple syrup with a touch of bourbon. When buying jarred herbs and spices, always check the expiration date. This recipe makes about five pancakes.

Candied Pecans or Pumpkin Seeds (page 19)

¼ cup all-purpose flour

2 tablespoons stoneground yellow cornmeal

1 teaspoon pumpkin pie spice mix (see Note on page 19)

½ teaspoon baking powder

¼ teaspoon salt

⅓ cup whole milk

¼ cup canned pumpkin purée

1 large egg

1 teaspoon firmly packed dark brown sugar

1 tablespoon melted unsalted butter or vegetable oil

¼ teaspoon vanilla extract

1½ tablespoons dried cranberries

Canola or other vegetable oil, for cooking the pancakes

Maple syrup, warmed, with a little bourbon stirred in (optional)

Make the Candied Pecans or Pumpkin Seeds if using.

In a bowl, whisk together the flour, cornmeal, pumpkin pie spice mix, baking powder, and salt. In another bowl, beat the milk, pumpkin, egg, brown sugar, butter, and vanilla until smooth. Stir the pumpkin mixture along with the cranberries into the dry ingredients until blended.

Heat a 10-inch cast-iron skillet or griddle over medium heat until hot but not smoking. Add enough oil to cover the bottom. Ladle the batter by ¼-cupfuls into the skillet and cook until small bubbles form on the surface and the bottoms are lightly browned, about 3 minutes per side. Turn and cook the second side until browned. Add a little more oil, if needed. Serve with Candied Pecans and maple syrup.

CANDIED PECANS OR PUMPKIN SEEDS

¼ cup chopped pecans or shelled roasted pumpkin seeds
1 tablespoon dark or light brown sugar
1 teaspoon water
¼ teaspoon salt
⅛ teaspoon pumpkin pie spice

In a nonstick skillet, combine the pecans, sugar, water, salt, and spice mixture. Cook over medium heat until the sugar melts and thickens, stirring often. It will take very little time. Transfer to a bowl and separate the nuts as the caramel cools and hardens.

Note: If you prefer to make your own pumpkin pie mixture, combine ½ teaspoon cinnamon, ¼ teaspoon ground ginger, ¼ teaspoon ground nutmeg, and a pinch of allspice.

MATZO *BREI* WITH CARAMELIZED ONIONS AND MUSHROOMS

My friend and fellow foodie Andrea Sperling uses the cast-iron skillet her father inherited from his mother. Andrea says matzo brei *(fried matzo) can be prepared many ways but, like most traditional foods, aficionados are generally partial to how their grandmother or mother made it, even if it was soggy and tasteless. Her dad used to say the secret of good fried matzo is a good cast-iron pan.*

Depending on which part of Europe your ancestors came from, matzo brei can be either sweet or savory. The savory version is traditionally made with chicken fat (schmaltz) and a lot of salt and pepper. To make her version more contemporary, Andrea substituted olive oil and butter for the chicken fat and added sautéed onions and mushrooms. It's delicious and far more than the sum of its few parts. Andrea says her family likes large portions, but for those with smaller appetites, this recipe will serve two to three.

1½ tablespoons unsalted butter

1 medium onion, sliced lengthwise into about ⅛-inch strips

5 ounces white mushrooms, wiped, trimmed, and sliced

3 unsalted matzos, broken into bite-sized pieces

3 large eggs, beaten

1 tablespoon extra-virgin olive oil

Salt and freshly ground black pepper

1 tablespoon chopped flat-leaf parsley, for garnish

In a 10-inch cast-iron skillet, melt the butter over medium-low heat. Add the onion and sauté until brown and caramelized, 8 to 10 minutes, stirring often. Add the mushrooms, raise the heat to medium, and continue stirring until they are lightly browned, about 5 minutes.

As the onion finishes cooking, soak the matzos in a bowl of warm water for about 3 minutes to become pliable; drain well. If still rigid, soak a little longer. Stir the eggs into the bowl.

Add the remaining butter and olive oil to the pan along with the matzos and stir to coat. Cook over medium-high heat until the pieces are browned in spots, about 10 minutes. Pour in the matzo-egg mixture and cook, turning often, mixing the onions and mushrooms with the matzos and eggs until done to your taste. Season to taste with salt and pepper. Serve garnished with chopped parsley.

SOUTH-OF-THE-BORDER STRATA

To celebrate our country's diversity, I made this Mexican-inspired version of a classic American strata in which bread soaked in milk and eggs is topped with layered leftovers and cheese. This traditional brunch dish often includes bacon and other meats, but many Mexicans base their diet on beans, corn, and peppers, so I chose this healthy and satisfying option. Like a frittata, bread pudding, or crustless quiche, it invites your own inventions.

1 large egg
3 tablespoons milk
½ teaspoon hot or mild chili powder according to taste
⅛ teaspoon kosher salt or sea salt, plus additional salt to season the layers
¾ cup day-old bread or roll, such as sourdough or rustic, torn into 1-inch pieces
1 teaspoon olive oil
1 medium shallot, chopped
¼ cup diced red bell pepper
Freshly ground black pepper
¼ cup drained and rinsed canned black beans
¼ cup fresh, frozen, or canned corn kernels
½ teaspoon ground cumin
½ (10-ounce) box frozen leaf spinach, defrosted, squeezed dry, and quickly steamed or sautéed in 1 teaspoon olive oil
½ teaspoon minced pickled jalapeño, if desired
⅓ cup shredded *queso blanco,* sharp cheddar, or Monterey Jack, or a mixture
Chopped cilantro leaves, for garnish
Hot sauce like Tabasco or Cholula, if desired

In a small bowl, beat together the egg, milk, chile powder, and salt. Add the bread and soak until the milk is absorbed, about 20 minutes, turning a few times.

Heat a 6-inch cast-iron skillet over medium heat until hot but not smoking. Add the oil, shallot, and red pepper and sauté until the shallot is lightly browned, 3 to 4 minutes, turning occasionally. Transfer to a bowl, season with salt and pepper, and set aside.

Spoon the soaked bread evenly into the skillet, and spread the onion-pepper mixture over it. Mix the black beans and corn together, season with salt, pepper, and cumin; add to the pan. Finally, combine the spinach and jalapeño pepper (if using), seasoning it lightly with salt and pepper. Cover the pan with foil or a lid and set aside for 20 minutes for the flavors to meld.

Preheat the oven to 350°F. Heat the pan over medium heat for 3 minutes, then transfer to the oven, and bake for 15 minutes. Remove the foil or lid, sprinkle on the cheese, and bake until golden brown, bubbling at the edges, and slightly puffed, about 15 minutes longer. Remove, let stand for 10 minutes, sprinkle on the cilantro, and serve with hot sauce (if using).

BOOZY BAILEYS IRISH CREAM FRENCH TOAST

The Baileys Irish Cream affair in our house began while my daughter was in high school and within three years we had several exchange students from The Haberdashers' School, in Hertfordshire, England. The first one brought me a large bottle of Baileys and word must have gone around that I liked it, as each successive student followed suit. Up to my eyeballs in the liqueur, I made a mousse, an ice cream, and this indulgent French toast with stale brioche for a "grown-up" friend. It's slightly crunchy on the outside and custardy inside.

Serve it with fresh berries mixed with a little orange juice to dress up the dish. Bacon or sausages are the logical partners in the morning, but this version could also be a decadent dessert at night. Soaking times can vary depending on how dry the bread is. The egg-bread mixture can also be refrigerated and soaked overnight.

2 large eggs
1 (50ml bottle) Baileys Irish Cream
½ cup half-and-half or milk
1¼ tablespoons granulated sugar
2 teaspoons pumpkin pie spice mix or make your own (see Note on page 19)
1 teaspoon vanilla
Pinch salt
2 (1-inch) thick slices stale brioche or challah
1 tablespoon unsalted butter
Confectioners' sugar, to garnish
1 cup sliced strawberries or raspberries
Sugar
Orange juice
Maple syrup (optional)

In a large flat bowl or pie plate, stir together the eggs, Baileys Irish Cream, half-and-half or milk, sugar, pumpkin pie spice mix, vanilla, and salt. Add the bread slices, turning to coat with the mixture, and soak until the liquid is just about absorbed, turning a couple of times, 1 to 1½ hours, depending how dry and large the slices are.

Preheat the oven to 350°F.

Once the bread is soaked, heat a 10-inch cast-iron skillet over medium-high heat. Add the butter, swirl to cover the bottom of the pan, add the bread slices, turn the heat to medium, and cook until golden brown, about 1 to 2 minutes per side, turning once. Transfer to the oven and bake until the toast is puffed and creamy in the center, about 7 minutes.

Meanwhile, combine the strawberries, a little sugar depending on how sweet the berries are, and a tablespoon of orange juice; turn to coat. Serve the French toast dusted with a little confectioners' sugar and the strawberries spooned on top. Add maple syrup, if desired.

SMOKED TROUT-GRUYÈRE QUICHE IN CORNMEAL CRUST

The marriage of smoked trout and Gruyère in this toothsome cornmeal-crusted quiche makes a delightful dish at almost any time of the day or evening. Dill, thyme, Dijon mustard, and horseradish add complexity and style to the taste.

If time is short, you can use a store-bought deep-dish pie shell and make it look homemade by defrosting the pastry until soft enough to crimp the edges. Because smoked trout can be salty, it's best to taste a bite first, as you may not need to add salt.

The quiche can be reheated in an oven but not a microwave because the crust will become soggy.

CRUST
¾ cup all-purpose flour
3 tablespoons stoneground yellow cornmeal
½ teaspoon sugar
¼ teaspoon sea salt
6 tablespoons chilled unsalted butter, cut into small cubes
2–2½ tablespoons ice water

FILLING
2 tablespoons unsalted butter, plus 1 teaspoon to sauté the shallot
1 medium shallot, thinly sliced
1 small Yukon Gold or red potato, scrubbed and cut into ¼-inch dice (about ⅓ cup)
2 large eggs
¾ cup half-and-half
3 ounces skinned smoked trout, flaked (about 1 fillet)

¾ cup (3 ounces) shredded Gruyère or Swiss cheese, divided
1 tablespoon prepared white horseradish
2 teaspoons Dijon mustard
1 tablespoon chopped dill leaves or 1 teaspoon dried
1 teaspoon dried thyme leaves
Finely grated zest of 1 small lemon
⅛–¼ teaspoon kosher salt or sea salt (optional)
Freshly ground black pepper

In a food processor fitted with a steel blade, combine the flour, cornmeal, sugar, and salt; pulse to blend. Add the butter and pulse until the mixture resembles coarse meal. Add 2 tablespoons of water and pulse until the mixture just comes together. If it is too crumbly and it doesn't stick together when a small amount is pinched between your fingers, slowly add the remaining water and pulse a few more times. Remove the dough, pat into a disk, and dust with flour. Cover with plastic wrap and chill for 30 minutes.

(Directions continued on next page)

Meanwhile, in an 8-inch cast-iron skillet, melt the teaspoon of butter over medium heat. Add the shallot, sauté until golden, 3 to 4 minutes, stirring once or twice, and transfer to a small bowl. Do not wipe out the pan. In a small saucepan of boiling water, blanch the potato cubes until almost tender, 3 to 4 minutes. Drain and add to the shallot.

Remove the dough from the refrigerator. On a lightly floured board, roll it into a 10-inch circle, sprinkling flour as needed. Fit it into the skillet (it will come almost up to the top of the pan), turn the top edge under, and crimp the edges; chill for 15 minutes.

Preheat the oven to 425°F.

Prick the crust all over with a fork. Bake for 15 minutes, then remove, and cool slightly. Adjust the temperature to 350°F.

In a large bowl, beat the eggs and half-and-half together. Gently stir in the shallot, potato, trout, ½ cup of the Gruyère, the horseradish, mustard, dill, thyme, lemon zest, salt, if using, and pepper to taste. Sprinkle on the remaining cheese and bake until a knife inserted in the center comes out almost clean, 30 to 35 minutes. Remove, let stand for 10 minutes, slice, and serve. Or serve at room temperature.

FONTINA, DRIED FIGS, PROSCIUTTO, AND CARAMELIZED ONION CROSTATA

This free-form tart, or crostata, makes a delectable appetizer or light lunch for two or three when combined with a green salad. The savory-sweet filling of fontina, caramelized onions, prosciutto, and figs is wrapped in a crust of mixed whole wheat and all-purpose flours.

Choose a mid-level fontina rather than a top-tier Italian import because they are less expensive and often melt better. You can also use purchased pizza dough to make this tart more quickly.

When a recipe calls for 6 tablespoons of flour or another dry ingredient, I find it faster to use ¼-cup and ⅛-cup metal measures.

CRUST
1 large egg
1 tablespoon cream, half-and-half,
    or milk
6 tablespoons all-purpose flour
    (see headnote)
6 tablespoons whole wheat flour
    (I prefer Bob's Red Mill)
Pinch salt
3 tablespoons cold unsalted
    butter, cut into small cubes
2 tablespoons ice water
½ teaspoon honey
1 teaspoon freshly squeezed
    lemon juice

For FILLING, see page 30

In a small bowl, beat the egg and cream together. Set aside.

In a mini food processor, combine the white and whole wheat flours and salt and pulse to blend. Add the butter and ice water and pulse into small pieces.

In a small bowl, blend 2½ tablespoons of the egg-cream mixture with the honey. (The remainder is used to glaze the crust.) Add it to the flour mixture and pulse until the dough resembles coarse meal. Add the lemon juice and pulse a few more times until the dough starts to pull together. Turn it out onto a floured board and knead briefly into a disk. Cover with plastic wrap and refrigerate for 2 hours or overnight.

Remove the dough from the refrigerator. On a floured workspace or pastry cloth, roll the dough into about an 11-inch circle. Transfer it to a cast-iron griddle pan or skillet and refrigerate while preparing the filling.

(Ingredients and Directions continued on next page)

FILLING

1½ teaspoons olive oil

1 small onion, thinly sliced onion

1 small clove garlic, minced

½ teaspoon dried thyme leaves

1 cup shredded fontina cheese

⅓ cup (about 6) dried black Mission figs, stems removed

2–3 thin slices prosciutto (about 1 ounce)

¼ teaspoon salt

Freshly ground black pepper

In a small skillet, heat the oil over medium-high heat until hot but not smoking. Add the onion, stirring to separate the pieces, reduce the heat to medium, and sauté until the onion is golden, 3 to 4 minutes, stirring often. Stir in the garlic and thyme and set aside to cool. Toss together with the cheese.

Preheat the oven to 400°F.

Remove the dough from the refrigerator. In a food processor or by hand, chop the figs and prosciutto into small pieces and spread them evenly over the crust, leaving about a 1¼-inch border. Cover with the cheese-onion mixture, add salt and pepper, and pleat the crust over the filling.

Brush the dough with the remaining egg mixture; avoid letting it drip onto the pan. Transfer to the middle of the oven and bake until the crust is golden brown and the cheese is bubbling, 20 to 23 minutes. Remove and let it stand for 15 minutes before cutting into slices.

DAY-AFTER-THANKSGIVING TURKEY HASH

This old-fashioned hash is great for a weekend breakfast or lunch, especially if you have leftover turkey (or even a purchased rotisserie chicken). It's got enough seasoning to lift the sautéed turkey, potato, onion, and corn mixture from the mundane to flavorful. Additions you might add include minced pickled jalapeños and crumbled cheese.

⅔ cup peeled and diced yam or scrubbed Yukon Gold potato

1 cup cooked turkey, shredded or cut into small cubes

⅓ cup fresh, defrosted frozen, or canned corn kernels

1 small shallot, finely chopped

1 tablespoon finely chopped flat-leaf parsley

1 teaspoon Worcestershire sauce

¼ teaspoon dry mustard

¼ teaspoon dried thyme leaves

Sea salt

Freshly ground black pepper

1 tablespoon unsalted butter

1+ tablespoon canola or other vegetable oil

¼ cup dry vermouth

2–3 poached or fried eggs (optional)

Fill a small saucepan halfway with salted water and bring to boil. Add the yam or potato and boil until the cubes are just cooked through, about 3 minutes; drain and leave in a strainer to dry.

In a bowl, combine the turkey, corn, shallot, parsley, Worcestershire sauce, dry mustard, thyme, and salt and pepper to taste. Add the potato and mix well.

Heat an 8-inch cast-iron skillet over medium heat until hot but not smoking. Add the butter and 2 teaspoons of the vegetable oil. Spoon in the hash mixture, flatten slightly with a spatula, and cook until it starts to brown on the bottom and become crusty, 10 to 15 minutes. Turn with a spatula, scraping up the browned bits, adding more oil if needed, and cook until the second side is browned, 6 to 8 minutes longer.

Pour on the vermouth and cook for 1 minute more. Serve on warm plates with eggs on top, if desired.

2. Lighter Fare,
Including Appetizers, Sandwiches & Pasta

TUSCAN WHITE BEAN–CHEESE DIP WITH PANCETTA AND SAGE

Here's a casual hors d'oeuvre to enjoy while preparing dinner or, as my friend, Chef Sara Comerford suggests, as a light meal combined with an arugula, fennel, and Parmesan salad with lemon vinaigrette.

Puréed cannellini beans, fontina and Parmigiano-Reggiano cheeses, pancetta, and sage warmed in a cast-iron skillet become a tasty dip that partners well with grilled or toasted Italian bread brushed with olive oil and rubbed with garlic. And to drink? Perhaps a crisp glass of chilled Orvieto, a light Chianti, or even a not-too-sweet Riesling.

The dip can be gently reheated in the pan with a little broth added, if needed.

For beans that get puréed, I generally buy canned beans, like Goya and Progresso brands, because I find they're better tasting and the texture is superior to many dried ones that are often old and end up tasteless. If the can says "no salt," you will need to season this dip to your taste.

¾ cup undrained canned cannellini or other white beans
2 tablespoons vegetable or chicken broth
3 tablespoons small cubes pancetta
⅓ cup shredded creamy fontina (not aged)
1½ tablespoons grated Parmigiano-Reggiano
½ tablespoon extra-virgin olive oil
½ tablespoon finely chopped sage leaves
Coarsely ground black pepper
Salt (optional)
Thin slices lightly toasted Italian bread rubbed with garlic and brushed with olive oil

In a mini food processor, purée the cannellini and broth until smooth, scraping down the sides a few times. Scrape into a 6-inch cast-iron skillet set over medium-low heat. Stir in the pancetta and cheeses until melted, followed by the olive oil and sage leaves. Season to taste with pepper and, if needed, salt. Serve warm with grilled bread slices.

ASIAN NOODLE SALAD WITH CRAB CAKES

When this colorful Asian noodle salad is dressed with tangy-sweet peanut vinaigrette and crowned with crunchy crab cakes, it rises to a festive level. With plenty of ingredients to add flavor, there are minimal additions to the crab so its sweet taste shines through. Enjoy it as a main course for lunch or dinner or as an appetizer for three.

Backfin crabmeat is a good option here because it's about half the price of jumbo lump meat, tastes delicious, and doesn't need to be broken apart for mixing. For the noodles, I get a box with four individually wrapped 3-ounce packets. The remaining packets will keep for a long time in your cupboard.

I recently discovered that Old Bay Seasoning comes in a lower-sodium version that is plenty salty for this dish.

CRAB CAKES
½ pound backfin crabmeat
¾ cup panko, divided
¼ cup finely chopped scallions or
    chives
Freshly ground black pepper
2 tablespoons mayonnaise
1 teaspoon freshly squeezed
    lemon juice
1 teaspoon Old Bay lower-sodium
    seasoning
1 large egg, beaten
3 tablespoons canola oil

For VINAIGRETTE and SALAD, see page 40.

In a medium bowl, pick through the crabmeat to remove any pieces of cartilage. Add ½ cup of the panko, scallions, and black pepper and toss gently. Set aside.

In a small bowl, blend the mayonnaise, lemon juice, Old Bay seasoning, and egg. Gently fold in the crab and form into six round cakes about ¾-inch thick. Pour the remaining quarter cup of panko into a flat dish. Gently press both sides of the crab cakes into the crumbs to coat. Place them on a dish, cover, and refrigerate for at least 2 hours. (You can make them a day before.)

Meanwhile, make the Asian Vinaigrette and Asian Noodle Salad (page 40).

When ready to serve the salad: Heat a 10-inch cast-iron skillet over medium-high heat until hot but not smoking. Add the oil. When it shimmers, add the crab cakes, and cook until golden brown, 3–4 minutes, turn once, and cook the other side until golden. Transfer to paper towels to drain.

(Directions continued on next page)

ASIAN VINAIGRETTE

2 tablespoons chunky peanut butter
2 tablespoons dark sesame oil
1 tablespoon freshly squeezed lime juice
½ tablespoon rice wine vinegar
½ tablespoon Thai fish sauce
2 teaspoons firmly packed dark brown sugar
1 teaspoon minced fresh ginger root
1 clove garlic, minced
Red pepper flakes (optional)

ASIAN NOODLES SALAD

1 (3-ounce) package udon noodles
½ cup sugar snap peas, strings removed, if needed
⅓ cup sliced scallions, including most of the green parts
¼ cup thinly sliced radishes
¼ cup sliced canned water chestnuts, drained
2 tablespoons chopped cilantro leaves
1 tablespoon coarsely chopped toasted peanuts, for garnish

In a small bowl, whisk together the peanut butter, sesame oil, lime juice, vinegar, fish sauce, brown sugar, ginger, and garlic. Stir in the red pepper flakes, if using. Cover and refrigerate until needed.

Cook the noodles according to the package directions. Drain and cool. Blanch the sugar snap peas in boiling salted water, drain, shock under cold water, and blot dry. In a wide bowl, combine the noodles, sugar snap peas, scallions, radishes, and water chestnuts.

If the vinaigrette is too thick, stir in a few drops of warm water. Pour over the salad and toss gently to coat evenly, adding a little more sesame oil, if needed. Divide between two large flat bowls, add the crab cakes, sprinkle the remaining cilantro leaves and toasted peanuts over the top, and serve.

GRILLED SWISS CHEESE AND BACON SANDWICH WITH BEER-GLAZED ONIONS

This melted Swiss (or cheddar) cheese and bacon sandwich, topped with a tangle of caraway-scented, beer-glazed onions, reminds me of pub fare I've eaten while visiting England or Ireland. It's so earthy and inviting. Sometimes I sprinkle Spicy-Sweet Jalapeños (page 52) on the cheese before it's melted for a subtle burst of heat.

1½ teaspoons canola or other vegetable oil
1 medium onion, sliced
½ cup beer of choice
¼ teaspoon caraway seeds
Salt
Freshly ground black pepper
4 slices firm white or multigrain bread, not thin sliced
2 tablespoons honey mustard or Dijon mustard
2 slices bacon, cooked
2 ounces thinly sliced Swiss cheese or sharp cheddar, or ½ cup shredded cheese
1½ tablespoons unsalted butter, softened
Cornichons, for garnish

In a small skillet, heat the oil over medium-high heat. Add the onion and sauté until richly browned, about 5 minutes, stirring often. Add the beer and caraway seeds, raise the heat to high, and boil until the beer almost completely evaporates and coats the onions. Season to taste with salt and pepper. Keep warm.

Heat a 10-inch cast-iron griddle or skillet or over medium heat until hot but not smoking.

Meanwhile, lay the bread slices on a clean workspace in a single layer and spread each slice with mustard all the way to the edges. Place two slices of bacon on two of the slices and top with cheese. Cover the cheese with the remaining bread with the mustard side down, pressing slightly to adhere.

Spread half of the butter over the two sandwiches and lay them buttered-side down in the pan. Reduce the heat to medium-low. Spread the remaining butter on the unbuttered tops; cover with a lid that is slightly smaller than the pan, so the sandwich doesn't become soggy. Cook until the cheese is melted and bubbling, about 8 minutes, turning the sandwiches halfway through. Remove, cut in half on the diagonal, spoon the onions on top, garnish with cornichons, and serve.

(Continued on page 43)

BACON AND CHEESE SANDWICHES:
SOME DELICIOUS MARRIAGES

All varieties of melted cheese are among my favorite partners for bacon or cured pork. And why not? From creamy to sharp, they embrace the salty-sweet taste. Serve these sandwiches open-faced or with two slices of bread. Here are some favorites:

- Provolone topped with pancetta on thin slices of lightly toasted olive or rosemary bread brushed with garlic olive oil.
- Gruyère on toasted whole-grain bread, brushed with Dijon mustard, topped with strips of crisp bacon and chopped toasted almonds.
- Cabrales (Spanish sheep's milk blue cheese) with Serrano ham and a little quince paste on toasted raisin bread. (Other blue cheeses will also work.)
- Manchego cheese with cranberry chutney and pepper bacon on lightly toasted, thinly sliced dark bread.
- Muenster cheese broiled with sliced tomatoes and bacon on whole grain bread with Dijon mustard.

MOM'S MAC 'N' CHEESE WITH BACON

My mom made scrumptious macaroni and cheese in the cast-iron Dutch oven she received as a wedding present. With its creamy sauce, sautéed onions, paprika, and loads of sharp cheddar cheese, my siblings and I loved it, especially the crunchy-cheesy topping. When I added bacon to the filling, plus Parmesan and panko to the topping, the mac was attacked with a vengeance, thus getting the nickname of "macattacaroni." Leave out the bacon, or use turkey bacon, if you wish.

Mom served her mac 'n' cheese as a side dish, but this skillet of cheesy pasta could easily be a main course, perhaps with a tossed green salad on the side.

1 cup uncooked elbow macaroni, *cellentani,* or other tubular pasta
2 thick slices lean bacon, cut into ½-inch pieces (optional)
1 small onion, diced
1½ teaspoons unsalted butter
1 tablespoon all-purpose flour
1 cup whole milk
1¼ cups shredded sharp cheddar cheese, divided
¼ teaspoon sweet or hot paprika
¼ teaspoon salt or to taste
Freshly ground black pepper
2 tablespoons grated Parmigiano-Reggiano cheese
1½ tablespoons panko

Preheat the oven to 350°F. Bring a medium-sized saucepan half full of salted water to a boil. Add the pasta and cook until al dente, about 10 minutes; drain and set aside.

Meanwhile, put the bacon in a cold 6-inch cast-iron skillet and cook over medium heat until a little bacon fat covers the bottom of the pan, about 3 minutes. Stir in the onion and sauté until golden and the bacon is cooked through, about 4 minutes, stirring frequently. (If not using bacon, use a tablespoon butter or vegetable oil.)

Add enough butter to have 1 tablespoon of fat in the pan. When melted, stir in the flour and cook until lightly colored, about 3 minutes, stirring constantly. Slowly whisk in the milk and bring to a boil, stirring until smooth. Reduce the heat and simmer until the sauce thickens, 8 to 10 minutes, stirring regularly and scraping the edges with a silicone spatula. Add 1 cup of the cheese and stir until melted. Stir in the macaroni and season with paprika, salt, and pepper to taste.

In a bowl, combine the remaining cheddar with the Parmigiano-Reggiano and panko. Spoon the mixture over the macaroni and bake until the top is golden brown and bubbling, 20 to 25 minutes. If not brown enough, run under the broiler for a few minutes, watching carefully that it doesn't burn. Remove the skillet and cool for 5 minutes before serving.

MAC 'N' CHEESE WITH CHORIZO, TOMATOES, AND ADOBO SAUCE

This mac 'n' cheese is pure comfort food with a zesty Mexican bite. Chorizo, diced canned tomatoes, and adobo sauce are blended into Oaxaca or sharp cheddar cheese sauce to make it a hearty main course or a festive brunch option for two hungry eaters or perhaps a third. As the headnote to Thin-Crusted Mexican Pizza with Queso Oaxaca *and* Chorizo *on page 51 explains, the main difference between Spanish and Mexican chorizo sausages is that the Spanish version is sold cooked.*

1 cup uncooked elbow, penne, or other tubular pasta

1 teaspoon canola or other vegetable oil for the pan

2 links uncooked Mexican-style chorizo sausages, casing removed and broken into small pieces

1 small onion, diced

2 tablespoons all-purpose flour

1½ cups whole milk

1¼ cups shredded Oaxaca or sharp cheddar cheese, divided

½–1 teaspoon abodo sauce or to taste

⅓ cup petite diced, fire-roasted canned tomatoes, preferably with green chiles

¼ teaspoon sea salt

Freshly ground black pepper

2 tablespoons chopped cilantro leaves, for garnish

Cholula Hot Sauce, if desired

Preheat the oven to 400°F. Bring a medium-sized saucepan half full of salted water to a boil. Add the pasta and cook until al dente, about 10 minutes; drain and set aside.

Meanwhile, heat an 8-inch cast-iron skillet over medium heat until hot but not smoking. Add the oil and chorizo and cook until the sausage pieces are still slightly pink in the center, 3 to 4 minutes. Stir in the onion and cook until wilted. With a slotted spoon, transfer the chorizo and onion to a bowl and set aside.

Drain all but about 2 tablespoons of fat from the pan. Stir in the flour and cook until lightly colored, about 3 minutes, stirring constantly. Reduce the heat to medium-low, slowly whisk in the milk, and bring to a boil, stirring until smooth. Simmer the sauce until thickened, 6 to 8 minutes, scraping the bottom and sides with a silicone spatula several times. Stir in 1 cup of the cheese and adobo sauce to taste. Add the pasta, chorizo, onion, tomatoes, and salt and pepper to taste. Stir to mix well.

Cover the pan with foil or a lid and bake for 15 minutes. Uncover, sprinkle on the remaining cheese, and bake until the cheese is bubbling and nicely browned on top, 6 to 7 minutes. Remove the skillet and let stand for 5 minutes. Sprinkle with the cilantro leaves and serve with Cholula hot sauce, if desired.

NORTH AFRICAN SAUSAGE PIZZA IN PHYLLO

Inside this crunchy phyllo pizza are North African merguez blended with kalamata olives, sautéed onions, and feta cheese. The sausages are beautifully spicy, but adding a touch of harissa (Tunisian hot pepper paste) makes the filling even more enticing. Rather than melted butter, the phyllo layers are brushed with olive oil scented with cumin before being trimmed and turned over the meat filling.

½ tablespoon olive oil, plus 2 tablespoons to brush on the phyllo

1 small onion, thinly sliced

6 ounces *merguez* (lamb sausage), or a mix of lamb and pork sausage, casings removed, and coarsely chopped (I prefer D'Artagnan brand)

3 tablespoons pitted kalamata olives, chopped, plus 1 olive for the center

2 tablespoons chopped oven-dried tomatoes

1 tablespoon tomato paste

1 teaspoon dried oregano

⅛ teaspoon harissa (optional)

Kosher salt or sea salt (optional)

Freshly ground black pepper

½ teaspoon ground cumin

¼ cup crumbled feta

¼ cup shredded part-skim mozzarella

3 sheets phyllo, defrosted overnight, if frozen

Heat an 8-inch cast-iron skillet over medium heat until hot but not smoking. Add the ½ tablespoon of olive oil and onion and sauté until soft, 2 to 3 minutes. Stir in the sausage and sauté until just cooked through, 2 to 3 minutes, breaking up the pieces up with a wooden spatula. Using a slotted spoon, transfer the meat and onions to a bowl and mix in the olives, tomatoes, tomato paste, oregano, harissa, if using, about ¼ teaspoon salt, and pepper to taste.

Preheat the oven to 375°F. Stir the cumin into the remaining oil. Wipe out the pan and brush with a little of the oil.

In a small bowl, blend the feta and mozzarella and set aside.

Lay one sheet of phyllo on the workspace with the short edge near you. Brush lightly with the cumin oil and bring the bottom edge to the top. Fold the bottom to the top again and lay the piece across the center of the skillet with the long edges extending beyond the pan. Repeat with the remaining sheets, each time crossing the center and covering the bottom of the pan.

Scrape the meat mixture into the pan, and spoon on the cheeses. Trim the phyllo edges even with the top of the skillet and flip them over the cheese. Brush the edges with some of the oil.

Bake in the middle of the oven until crisp and golden brown, about 25 minutes. Remove, let stand for at least 5 minutes, then cut into quarters, and serve.

THIN-CRUSTED MEXICAN PIZZA WITH QUESO OAXACA AND CHORIZO

Thin-crusted pizza lovers: this south-of-the-border version with Mexican chorizo, Oaxaca cheese, onion, and red bell pepper is for you—especially if you like crunch and spice in your food. Years ago, I discovered that pizzas can be made almost at a moment's notice with a flour tortilla in a cast-iron griddle pan or skillet. Eat them right away so they don't get soggy. Another option is purchased pizza dough.

Mexican chorizo is made with uncooked ground pork seasoned with chile peppers. The Spanish version of the same name is already cooked. Be sure to taste a little of the cheese and a bite of cooked sausage to see how salty it is before adding more salt.

Vegetable or extra-virgin olive oil, to brush in the pan
1 (10-inch) flour tortilla
½ cup purchased or homemade pizza sauce
¾ cup coarsely shredded Oaxaca cheese or mozzarella
½ teaspoon dried oregano, preferably Mexican
Freshly ground black pepper
Pinch salt (optional)
1 large shallot or ½ small onion, very thinly sliced and separated into rings
¼ cup finely diced red bell pepper
1 tablespoon finely chopped pickled jalapeños, or more to taste (optional)
1 link uncooked Mexican-style chorizo sausage, casing removed and thinly sliced
3 tablespoons grated Cotija or Parmesan cheese

Position the oven rack about 7 inches from the heat and turn the broiler on to high.

Heat a 10-inch cast-iron skillet over medium-high heat until hot but not smoking, 3 to 4 minutes. Turn the heat to low and brush the pan lightly with oil. Lay the tortilla in the pan with the rougher side down. Cover the surface with pizza sauce almost to the edge and sprinkle on the shredded cheese mixture. Add the oregano, pepper, and salt, if using. Sprinkle on the onion, diced pepper, jalapeños (if using), and chorizo. Top with the Cotija cheese.

Broil until the sausage is cooked and the cheese is bubbling with little brown spots, 4 to 5 minutes. Run a spatula around the edges to loosen. If the bottom is not crisp and lightly browned, place the skillet on top of the stove over medium heat and continue cooking for 1 to 2 minutes, shaking the pan often. Remove to a cutting board, blot gently with paper towels if the sausage is greasy, cut into wedges, and enjoy.

SAUTÉED ONION-MUSHROOM AND SPICY-SWEET JALAPEÑO FLATBREAD

With its sautéed mushrooms and onions topped with Monterey Jack cheese, this flatbread looks familiar. What sets it apart and makes it addictive is the subtly spicy yet sweet note from a fresh jalapeño reduced in agave nectar, vinegar, and lime juice, then minced and mixed in the topping to perfume each bite. I like it fairly spicy, but remove the seeds and membranes for less heat. Enjoy it for hors d'oeuvres, lunch, or whenever you want a tasty nibble.

SPICY-SWEET JALAPEÑOS
1 medium-large jalapeño (about 3–4 inches), membranes and seeds removed, if desired, and diced
1½ tablespoon agave nectar or honey
1½ tablespoon apple cider vinegar
¼ teaspoon freshly squeezed lime juice

TOPPING
3 tablespoons extra-virgin olive oil, divided
1 small onion, sliced
8 ounces cremini mushrooms, wiped, trimmed, and sliced
1 large clove garlic, minced
¼ teaspoon dried oregano
¼ teaspoon salt
All-purpose flour
½ pound purchased or homemade pizza dough
½ cup coarsely shredded Monterey Jack cheese

In a 2-cup glass measure or bowl, combine the peppers, agave, and vinegar in a microwave and cook on high for 4 minutes. Remove, stir in the lime juice, cool, and chop fairly finely.

Place a 10-inch griddle or cast-iron skillet in the oven and preheat to 450°F.

While the griddle or pan is heating, in a large skillet, heat 1 tablespoon of the oil over medium-high heat. Add the onion and sauté until wilted, 2 to 3 minutes. Add the remaining oil and mushrooms, and sauté until richly browned, about 4 minutes, stirring often. Stir in the garlic, oregano, salt, and Spicy-Sweet Jalapeños including any liquid. Turn off the heat.

Dust the dough and workspace lightly with flour. Using a rolling pin, roll and stretch the dough into an 8-inch circle about ¼-inch thick. Brush the hot griddle with oil, add the dough, and carefully flatten it with your fingertips. Cook until golden brown in spots, about 2 minutes; using tongs, turn and cook the second side until browned in spots.

Brush the flatbread with a little oil. Spoon on the mushroom mixture, sprinkle with the Jack cheese, and transfer to the oven to bake until the cheese is melted and bubbling, 4 to 5 minutes. If desired, run briefly under the broiler to brown a bit more. Remove, let stand for 5 to 10 minutes, cut into wedges, and serve.

SMOKED DUCK-MONTEREY JACK CHEESE QUESADILLAS WITH MANGO-RED PEPPER SALSA

This stylish snack or light lunch allows your creativity to shine between two tortillas. Using a skillet or griddle, spread a tortilla with a little adobo sauce, honey mustard, or mole sauce. Sprinkle on cheese—such as Monterey Jack, cheddar, Gouda, or blue—and top with pickled jalapeños, grilled onions, or olives. You can also use different flavored tortillas. Spicy mango—red pepper salsa and pickled onions can also be found in many markets these days.

PICKLED RED ONIONS
2 tablespoons apple cider vinegar
1 small clove garlic, finely chopped
1 teaspoon granulated sugar
½ teaspoon salt
Small pinch red pepper flakes
¼ cup hot water
½ small red onion, very thinly sliced

MANGO-RED PEPPER SALSA
½ cup diced mango
½ diced small red bell pepper
¼ cup finely chopped red onion
2 tablespoons chopped cilantro leaves
1¼ teaspoons agave nectar, or more to taste
1–2 teaspoons pickled jalapeño juice
Freshly squeezed lime juice to taste
Sea salt

QUESADILLA
Canola or other vegetable oil, to brush the pan
2 (8-inch) flour tortillas
½ cup (2 ounces) coarsely shredded Manchego or Monterey Jack cheese
1½ ounces very thinly sliced smoked duck breast (I use D'Artagnan's)

In a glass jar or small bowl, combine the vinegar, garlic, sugar, salt, and red pepper flakes. Add the water, stir until the sugar dissolves, then add the onion. Stir a couple times, cover, and set aside for about an hour; refrigerate for up to three weeks.

In a small bowl, combine the mango, red pepper, onion, cilantro leaves, agave nectar, pickled jalapeño juices, and salt to taste. Set aside. Taste to adjust the flavors before serving.

Heat a 10-inch cast-iron skillet or griddle over medium heat. Brush with oil. Lay a tortilla in the pan, evenly sprinkle on half of the cheese, and add the duck. With a slotted spoon, remove about half of the pickled red onions, blot dry with paper towels, and sprinkle over the duck. Add the remaining cheese and the second tortilla; cook until the bottom is lightly browned, 3 to 4 minutes, pressing the top down with a spatula.

Turn and cook the second side until lightly colored and the cheese is melted, 2 to 3 minutes. Turn off the heat, cool slightly, cut into six wedges with a sharp knife or pizza cutter, and add a spoonful of the Mango—Red Pepper Salsa to each wedge.

FLAVORFUL BLACK BEAN BURGERS IN PITA POCKETS WITH HUMMUS AND *AJVAR*

Hamburger lovers who have become vegetarians will love these grilled Middle Eastern black bean burgers flavored with cumin and sumac, a wonderfully citrusy and salty spice made from ground berries that has no sodium. The burgers (pictured on page 210) are tucked inside pita pockets with hummus, ajvar, lettuce, and tomatoes. It's an appealing, healthy meal. Alternatively, you might also enjoy the Indian Tartar Sauce on page 107 on these burgers.

⅓ cup *Ajvar* (page 57) or purchased *ajvar*
1 cup canned black beans, rinsed and drained
¼ cup chopped onion
½ tablespoon chopped garlic
1 tablespoon chopped flat-leaf parsley
½ tablespoon ground cumin
½ tablespoon ground sumac
¼ teaspoon salt
⅛ teaspoon red pepper flakes
Freshly ground black pepper
1 large egg, beaten
⅓ cup panko, preferably whole wheat
Vegetable oil or nonstick cooking spray
2 small pita breads with pockets, preferably whole wheat, partially opened and warmed
⅓ cup prepared hummus
2 small romaine lettuce leaves
2 thin slices tomato
1 small red onion, thinly sliced and separated into rings

Prepare the *ajvar*, if making.

In a food processor, combine the black beans, onion, garlic, parsley, cumin, sumac, salt, red pepper flakes, and black pepper. Pulse until the mixture is chunky-smooth. Add the egg and panko and pulse just until blended but with small bits of beans still visible. The mixture, while a little sticky, should hold together. Gently form into two patties about an inch thick.

Heat a 10-inch cast-iron grill pan, griddle, or skillet over medium heat until hot but not smoking. Brush with oil, lay the burgers in the pan, turn the heat to medium-low, and cook for about 7 minutes without moving. Turn and cook the second side for the same amount of time.

Meanwhile, on the inside of each pita, spread some hummus on one side and *ajvar* on the other. Slide in the burgers, add the lettuce, tomato, and onion, and serve.

AJVAR

Makes about 1 cup

I love this roasted sweet pepper and eggplant condiment as a topping for black bean burgers, grilled cheese sandwiches, and even as a topping for sautéed skinless chicken thighs.

1 small eggplant (about ¾ pound)
1 large red bell pepper
1½ tablespoons extra-virgin olive oil
½ tablespoon freshly squeezed
    lemon juice or white vinegar
1 teaspoon tomato paste
1 clove garlic, finely chopped
Kosher salt or sea salt
Freshly ground black pepper
Dried red pepper flakes (optional)

Heat the oven to 475°F. Brush the eggplant and pepper with oil, place them in a 10-inch cast-iron skillet, and roast until their skins blister and turn black, about 30 minutes, turning often with tongs. Transfer to a heatproof bowl, cover with a clean towel or plastic wrap, and steam for 10 minutes; peel and discard the blackened skins, seeds, and membranes.

Transfer to a food processor and pulse until chunky smooth. Add the lemon juice, tomato paste, and garlic, and drizzle in the oil, pulsing several times to blend. Season to taste with salt, pepper, and red pepper flakes (if using). Scrape into a clean glass jar, cover, and refrigerate. It will keep for at least 1 week or longer.

GRILLED PORTOBELLO MUSHROOM CAPS
WITH *BURRATA* AND HEIRLOOM TOMATOES

There are layers of flavors and temperatures to discover in this celebration of summer's bounty. Earthy, warm grilled mushroom caps are filled with juicy, room temperature tomatoes and fresh basil, and then topped with creamy, slightly chilled burrata. *I prefer thicker mushrooms, as they are "meatier." You can also toss the tomatoes and* burrata *with sliced white mushrooms and basil for a lovely but simpler salad.*

4 tablespoons extra-virgin olive oil, plus oil to brush in the pan
1 small clove garlic, minced
2 teaspoons red wine vinegar
Kosher salt or coarse sea salt
Freshly ground black pepper
2 large portobello mushrooms (about 3 inches wide)
1–2 firm, ripe heirloom tomatoes, of any color, diced (about 6 ounces)
2 tablespoons finely chopped shallots
Julienned basil leaves, plus leaves for garnish
1 small *burrata* cheese, sliced
Basil oil (page 63) or additional extra-virgin olive oil
Few drops balsamic glaze

In a medium bowl, mix together 3 tablespoons of the olive oil, garlic, vinegar, and salt and pepper to taste.

Gently twist off the stems from the mushroom caps and remove the gills. Brush the mushrooms inside and outside with the oil mixture.

Combine the tomatoes and shallots with the remaining oil. Set aside.

Heat a cast-iron skillet over medium-high heat until hot but not smoking. Add a little oil to the pan, place the caps smooth-side down, and sauté until slightly softened and lightly colored, about 3 minutes. Turn and cook the second side for 3 minutes, cover, and cook until just softened when the tip of a small knife is inserted. The time will vary according to how thick the mushroom caps are. Transfer to plates.

Add the julienned basil leaves to the tomatoes and spoon them and their juices into the caps. Add the *burrata*, a drizzle of basil oil, if using, or more olive oil, and a few drops of balsamic glaze. Sprinkle with black pepper and a little more salt and serve.

VEGETARIAN CHILI OVER CHEESY GRITS

This robust chili includes a cornucopia of vegetables and beans simmered in a richly seasoned but not overly spicy broth. You can also add ground turkey or beef to make it heartier and cook the meat along with the vegetables. Raw shrimp may also be cooked this way, or you can reheat diced cooked chicken in the hot mixture. Be sure to have all the spices ready to add to the pan, as this goes quickly once you start. Serve over Cheesy Grits (page 62) or rice.

2 teaspoons canola or other vegetable oil
⅓ cup diced onion
1½ teaspoons chili powder, hot or mild to taste
1 teaspoon ground cumin
¼–½ teaspoon minced chipotle in adobo sauce
½ teaspoon dried oregano
1 teaspoon finely chopped jalapeño
1 large clove garlic, finely chopped
½ cup diced butternut squash
½ cup canned black beans, rinsed and drained
½ cup garbanzo beans, rinsed and drained
½ cup diced red bell pepper
½ cup diced canned tomatoes, including juice
⅔ cup vegetable broth
Kosher salt or sea salt and freshly ground black pepper
½ tablespoon fine cornmeal, if needed to thicken
Shredded soft Mexican cheese, like Oaxaca or Asadero, or cheddar cheese, for garnish
Roasted pumpkin seeds, for garnish
½ firm, ripe Hass avocado, diced, for garnish
2 tablespoons chopped cilantro leaves, for garnish

Heat an 8-inch cast-iron skillet over medium heat to hot but not smoking. Add the oil and the onions and sauté until wilted, about 3 minutes. Add the chili powder, cumin, chipotle, oregano, jalapeño, and garlic, and stir to blend.

Add the butternut squash, black beans, garbanzo beans, bell pepper, tomatoes, and vegetable broth. Stir to blend well. Bring to a boil, then reduce the heat, cover with a tight-fitting lid, and simmer until the vegetables are tender, about 30 minutes. If the chili is too soupy, stir in the cornmeal, and cook uncovered to thicken, about 5 minutes.

Season to taste with salt and pepper. Serve garnished with cheese, pumpkin seeds, avocado, and cilantro.

CHEESY GRITS

Grits, like hominy (see page 95), are a Native American corn product. The dried and processed corn kernels are coarsely ground on a stone mill. They're most popular in the South and Southwest. These cheesy grits would also make a great partner for spiced grilled shrimp or chicken.

⅔ cups vegetable or chicken broth
⅔ cups whole milk
⅓ cup coarse ground cornmeal
½ cup shredded sharp white or yellow cheddar cheese
1 teaspoon unsalted butter
Salt
Tabasco or other hot sauce (optional)

Combine the broth and milk in a small saucepan and bring a boil. Slowly add the cornmeal, stirring until blended and smooth. Turn the heat to low and simmer until the mixture is creamy, 25 to 30 minutes, stirring frequently with a silicone scraper to prevent the grits from sticking to the bottom of the pan. Remove from the heat, add the cheese and butter, and season to taste with salt and Tabasco, if using.

If the mixture gets thick and starts to dry out, stir in more liquid—water or broth by quarter-cupfuls—until smooth. Once the grits are done, stir in the butter and cheese and cook until melted. Season to taste with salt and Tabasco sauce, if desired, before serving.

WHAT TO DO WITH AN OVERABUNDANCE OF BASIL

In season, we find large bunches of basil. Alas, too much is often just that: more than we can use in a timely fashion. Why not make Basil Oil (below) with the leaves or the Quick Homemade Pesto on page 12

BASIL OIL

The amount of leftover basil you have can vary, so measure roughly half as much oil as the quantity of packed leaves that you have in a measuring cup, having first discarded the stems and any bruised leaves. The oil should be chilled and a bowl of ice water should be ready.

In a pot of boiling water, quickly blanch the leaves until wilted, 6 to 8 seconds, pour through a strainer, transfer to the ice water, and gently agitate until cold. Strain again and gently blot dry with paper towels.

In the jar of an electric blender, combine the leaves, oil, about ¼ teaspoon salt per cup of leaves; purée until smooth. Set aside for about 30 minutes, then pour through a strainer lined with cheesecloth, pressing with a silicone spatula or the back of a spoon to obtain as much oil as possible.

Pour into a clean jar and cover. Use at once or refrigerate for up to a week, returning the oil to room temperature before using.

3. Vegetables & Side Dishes

ROASTED ASPARAGUS
WITH PROSCIUTTO GREMOLATA

If you've never tasted asparagus roasted in cast iron, you're in for a treat. The spears become bright green with a few charred spots and gain a depth of flavor impossible to achieve by boiling or steaming. Here, they're topped with gremolata, an Italian mixture made with grated lemon, parsley, and garlic. I added a little prosciutto, as well.

2 very thin slices prosciutto, finely chopped (about ½ ounce)
2 tablespoons finely chopped flat-leaf parsley
1 teaspoon grated lemon zest
1 clove garlic, grated or minced
1 tablespoon extra-virgin olive oil, divided
½ pound medium asparagus spears, woody ends snapped off
Kosher salt or coarse sea salt
Freshly ground black pepper

In a small bowl, combine the prosciutto, parsley, lemon zest, garlic, and ½ tablespoon of the olive oil. Gently stir together, cover, and set aside.

Preheat the oven to 425°F.

Heat an 8- or 10-inch cast-iron skillet over medium-high heat. Add the remaining ½ tablespoon of oil and the asparagus and shake the pan to coat evenly. Sprinkle on about ¼ teaspoon of salt. Transfer the skillet to the oven and roast until the asparagus spears are bright green and crisp-tender with little char spots, 10 to 15 minutes, or more if you prefer them softer, shaking the pan occasionally. Remove, sprinkle with the gremolata and black pepper, if desired, and serve.

BROCCOLI RABE (RAPINI) SPANAKOPITA

Decades ago, Greek spinach pie, or spanakopita, was considered exotic. I still like greens in a flaky crust but made this version more of a global fusion side dish. I thought rapini was more contemporary than spinach, replaced the abundant butter with less olive oil, and used Parmigiano-Reggiano instead of feta. It's baked and served in a fluted dish made with a tortilla. The bright greens are framed by a narrow band of Parmigiano custard. You can use leftover tortillas for quesadillas (page 169), make spicy fried taco chips, and dunk them in a variety of hot and cold dips, like the Tuscan White Bean–Cheese Dip with Pancetta and Sage on page 37.

Olive oil to brush on the tortilla and skillet, plus 1 tablespoon to sauté the rapini
1 (8-inch) flour tortilla
Kosher salt or sea salt
7–8 ounces broccoli rabe, coarse stems trimmed off and roughly chopped (about 7 cups)
1 large clove garlic, finely chopped
4 tablespoons grated Parmigiano-Reggiano, divided
1 large egg, beaten
Grated zest of 1 small lemon
Generous pinch red pepper flakes
Freshly ground black pepper

Preheat the oven to 375°F. Lightly brush a 6-inch cast-iron skillet with oil. Lay the tortilla in the pan, pressing the edges into the corners so the edges are slightly rippled, and brush lightly with oil. Transfer to the oven and bake until lightly colored on the edges with some brown spots on the bottom of the tortilla, 10 to 12 minutes. If the middle swells up, prick with the tip of a knife and press flat. Remove from the oven, lift from the pan, and let cool. Leave the oven on.

Meanwhile, bring a medium-sized saucepan half full of water to a boil. Add a generous pinch of salt and the broccoli rabe, boil until wilted, about 2 minutes, pour into a large strainer, shock under cold water, and drain well.

In the cast-iron skillet, heat 1 tablespoon of oil over medium-high heat. Add the broccoli rabe and garlic and sauté until tender but still bright green, and the stems are almost cooked through, 2 to 3 minutes, turning often. Scrape into a bowl and cool for a few

(Directions continued on next page)

minutes. Wipe out the skillet, brush lightly with oil, and return the tortilla shell to the pan.

Add 3 tablespoons of the Parmigiano-Reggiano, the egg, lemon zest, salt, if needed, red pepper flakes, and black pepper to the broccoli rabe and mix well. Scrape into the tortilla shell, sprinkle on the final tablespoon of cheese, and bake until the egg is set and a knife tip inserted in the center comes out clean, 18 to 20 minutes. Remove, let stand for 5 minutes, cut in half, and serve.

ROASTED CORN PANCAKES WITH CHERRY TOMATO SALSA AND GOAT CHEESE

Makes 5–6 (3-inch) pancakes

I love these pancakes made with fresh-off-the-cob roasted corn topped with juicy Cherry Tomato Salsa (heirlooms if you can find them) and tangy goat cheese sprinkled on top. It's a celebration of summertime's bounty. The combination makes a great brunch or lunch.

Corn roasted in a cast-iron skillet turns the kernels bright yellow and intensifies the flavor. No fresh corn? Sauté defrosted frozen or even good-quality canned kernels for a few minutes in a little hot oil, turning a couple times, until lightly colored. It's not the same as fresh summer corn, but it's pretty darn wonderful.

Cherry Tomato Salsa (page 73)
Canola or other vegetable oil for the
   skillet
Kernels from 1 large ear corn, about
   ½ cup, or canned or defrosted frozen
   kernels (See page 73 for how to
   remove the kernels)
½ cup lowfat buttermilk
1 tablespoon melted unsalted butter or
   vegetable oil
1 large egg
¼ cup yellow cornmeal (I prefer Bob's
   Red Mill coarse grind)
¼ cup all-purpose flour
1 teaspoon baking powder
¼ teaspoon sugar
¼ teaspoon salt
⅛ teaspoon baking soda
Freshly ground black pepper
1 tablespoon julienned basil leaves
2–3 tablespoons crumbled goat cheese,
   to garnish

Prepare the Cherry Tomato Salsa. Cover and set aside in a cool spot while making the pancakes.

Heat a 10-inch cast-iron skillet over medium-high heat until hot but not smoking. Brush with a little oil, add the corn, and sauté until some charred spots appear, 4 to 5 minutes, stirring once or twice. Set aside to cool.

In a small bowl, whisk the buttermilk, butter or oil, and egg together. In another bowl, stir together the cornmeal, flour, baking powder, sugar, salt, baking soda, and black pepper to taste. Using a silicone spatula, scrape the wet mixture along with the corn and basil into the dry ingredients and mix just until blended. Cover and refrigerate for 30 minutes.

(Directions continued on page 73)

Heat the skillet over medium-high until hot but not smoking. Add a little oil. Using a ¼-cup metal measure or a 2-ounce standard ice cream scoop, ladle a scant quarter-cup of batter into the skillet. You will need to do this in two batches.

Reduce the heat to medium and cook until bubbles form on the surface and the bottoms are golden, 2 to 3 minutes, turn, and cook the second sides until done. Remove, cook the remaining pancakes, and serve with Cherry Tomato Salsa and goat cheese sprinkled on top.

To remove corn kernels from the cobs without having them fly all over:

Shuck the ear and remove the silk. Put the cob in a deep bowl with the pointed end down. Slice down the four sides, turning a quarter turn each time, and let the kernels fall into the bowl, separating them into individual kernels.

Cherry Tomato Salsa

2 cups (1 dry pint) cherry tomatoes, halved
2 large scallions, including most of the green parts, finely chopped
3 tablespoons julienned basil leaves
1½ tablespoons extra-virgin olive oil
2 teaspoons apple cider vinegar or freshly squeezed lime juice
Kosher salt or coarse sea salt
Freshly ground black pepper

In a medium bowl, combine the tomatoes, scallions, and basil leaves. Drizzle on the oil and vinegar, season to taste with salt and pepper, toss, and refrigerate for about an hour. Taste to adjust the flavors.

LAVENDER-HONEY ROASTED BUTTERNUT SQUASH

I adore this delightful and easy vegetable dish with a surprise hint of dried lavender flowers. You can find small packets of them in better markets, herb stores, and bath shops. For a slightly more substantial dish, sprinkle on a little crumbled feta once the squash is tender. I add a pinch of crushed lavender just before serving to pop up the flavor. A final sprinkle of Maldon Salt or other large flakes of salt makes the flavors sparkle more.

2 cups (8 ounces) medium-sized pieces butternut squash
1 tablespoon unsalted butter, cut in small cubes
2 teaspoons honey
¼ teaspoon dried lavender flowers, plus a pinch to add before serving
¼ teaspoon dried thyme leaves
Kosher salt or sea salt
Pinch white pepper
2 tablespoons crumbled feta (optional)
Maldon Salt or other large-flake sea salt (optional)

Preheat the oven to 400°F.

In an 8-inch cast-iron skillet, combine the squash, butter, honey, lavender and thyme leaves, salt, and white pepper, turning to coat evenly. Roast until richly glazed and tender when pricked with a knife, about 25 minutes, turning a few times.

Remove from the oven, sprinkle on a pinch of crushed lavender and feta, if using, plus some large flakes of sea salt, and serve.

ZESTY CAULIFLOWER, PINE NUTS, AND CURRANTS WITH TAHINI-YOGURT SAUCE

Roasted cauliflower tossed with pine nuts and currants and drizzled with tahini-yogurt sauce makes an enticing side dish with sweet-hot Aleppo pepper adding a ribbon of flavor throughout. If the head of cauliflower you bought for the Oven-Roasted Shrimp, Cauliflower, and Cherry Tomatoes recipe on page 109 was large, and you have a couple cups of florets left over, here's an ideal place to use them.

Thanks to my dear friend Françoise Horowicz for suggesting using a Microplane zester to grate garlic cloves.

CAULIFLOWER
2–2½ cups cauliflower florets
1 tablespoons olive oil
¼–½ teaspoon kosher salt or coarse sea salt
¼ teaspoon Aleppo pepper flakes, divided
1½ tablespoon pine nuts, lightly toasted
1½ tablespoons dried currants, plumped in warm water if not soft

TAHINI-YOGURT SAUCE
¼ cup full-fat Greek yogurt
¼ cup tahini, well-stirred
1 large clove garlic, minced or grated (see headnote)
1–1½ tablespoons freshly squeezed lemon juice
1 tablespoon extra-virgin olive oil
Warm water to thin the sauce, as needed
Julienned mint leaves, to garnish

Put an 8-inch cast-iron skillet in the oven and preheat to 425°F.

In a large bowl, stir together the cauliflower, oil, salt, and ⅛ teaspoon Aleppo pepper. Scrape into the heated skillet in an even layer and return to the middle of the oven. Roast until the florets are lightly browned and almost tender, 20 to 25 minutes, turning occasionally.

Meanwhile, in a bowl, whisk together the yogurt, tahini, garlic, lemon juice, and olive oil. Add warm water to thin to a sauce consistency, if needed. Season to taste with salt and pepper.

Remove the cauliflower from the oven, sprinkle on the pine nuts and currants, and gently turn to mix. Drizzle the sauce on top, and serve with the mint leaves and the remaining Aleppo pepper sprinkled on top.

SEPHARDIC FRIED EGGPLANT WITH SESAME SEEDS, MINT, AND HONEY

While visiting Spain with my kids, I learned that the Moors introduced eggplant into the Iberian Peninsula sometime after the eighth century. Spanish Jews, or Sephardim, embraced the fruit and used it in many dishes. In Seville, these tantalizing, sweet and savory fried slices are a favorite tapa or vegetable side dish. Honey, mint, and sesame seeds are often used together in Arabic cooking.

1 small Italian eggplant (about 8 ounces), peeled and cut crosswise into ¼-inch-thick slices
Kosher salt or coarse sea salt
1 large egg, beaten
⅓ cup whole milk
½ cup all-purpose flour
Olive oil, ideally from Spain, for frying
1 tablespoon honey, preferably not very flowery-tasting, warmed
1 tablespoon roasted hulled sesame seeds
1 tablespoon julienned fresh mint leaves

In a large bowl, sprinkle the eggplant with about a teaspoon of salt, cover with cold water, and soak for 30 minutes. Drain, rinse, and pat dry on clean towels.

Turn the oven to warm. Beat the egg in a small flat bowl. Pour the milk into a second bowl. Add the flour to a flat bowl and season with a little salt.

Clip a deep fat/candy thermometer to the side of an 8- or 10-inch cast-iron skillet and pour in enough oil to measure ½ inch deep. Heat over medium-high heat until the oil measures 350°F. Alternatively, heat the oil until a small piece of bread dropped into the oil browns quickly.

Dip each eggplant slice briefly into the egg, letting any excess fall back into the bowl; next, dip it in the milk, and finally in the flour. Carefully slide the slices in the hot oil, taking care not to crowd them, and cook until golden brown on the first side, about 1 minute. Using a spatula, turn and cook the second side until golden. Remove with tongs to a platter lined with paper towels and continue with the remaining eggplant. Transfer to the oven while finishing the other slices.

Once all the slices have been fried, transfer them to a clean platter and season with salt. Drizzle with warm honey, sprinkle with sesame seeds and mint, and serve.

SWEET POTATO PANCAKES WITH ASIAN BRUSSELS SPROUTS SLAW

Several years ago, I judged a hazelnut recipe contest in Istanbul. (Turkey produces more than half of the world's supply of the nut.) The winner was a large sweet potato rösti with candied nuts and an apricot glaze. Since then, I've made several sweet potato pancakes but prefer to buy what are labeled yams. One of my favorite versions is this crunchy fried pancake topped with shaved Brussels sprouts, sesame seed, and dried cranberry slaw in tangy Asian Vinaigrette. Serve it as a side dish to accompany grilled sausages, roast chicken, or as an appetizer

Asian Brussels Sprouts Slaw
   (page 81)

PANCAKES
1¼ cup (about 4½ ounces) coarsely shredded yam or sweet potato
1 tablespoon finely chopped scallion, plus a few thin slices for garnish
1 large egg, beaten
1½ tablespoons coarse yellow cornmeal (I prefer Bob's Red Mill)
¼ teaspoon kosher salt or coarse sea salt
Canola or other vegetable oil, for frying

Prepare the Asian Brussels Sprouts Slaw.

Using a box grater or food processor fitted with a shredding disk, grate the yam or sweet potato. In a bowl, combine the yam, scallion, egg, cornmeal, and salt; using a fork, lightly toss to blend well.

Heat a 10-inch cast-iron skillet over medium-high heat until hot but not smoking. Add enough oil to measure ¼ inch deep. Using a soupspoon, scoop up half of the mixture and carefully add it to the skillet in about a 3½-inch circle. Repeat with the remaining mixture. Reduce the heat to medium and cook until the pancakes are golden brown on the first side, about 4 minutes, watching that they do not burn. Turn and cook the second side until browned, about the same time.

Remove with a spatula and blot on paper towels. The pancakes may be kept warm in a low oven for at least an hour. When ready to serve, spoon the Brussels Sprout Slaw on top.

Asian Brussels Sprouts Slaw

The vinaigrette and blanched cabbage may be prepared separately a day ahead of time.

DRESSING
Yields ¼ cup (You will use about half of it)
1 tablespoon hoisin sauce
1 tablespoon seasoned rice vinegar
1 teaspoon Japanese-style soy sauce, plus a few
   drops more to taste
Few drops chili oil, to taste
2 teaspoons minced fresh ginger root
2 tablespoons toasted sesame oil

SLAW
1½ cups (1½ ounces) loosely packed shredded
   Brussels sprouts, root ends trimmed, thinly
   sliced by hand or in a food processor fitted
   with a 2-mm slicing blade
1 large scallion, finely chopped, including most
   of the green part
1 tablespoon dried cranberries
1 tablespoon roasted hulled sesame seeds
Freshly ground black pepper

In a small bowl, stir together the hoisin sauce, vinegar, soy sauce, chili oil, and ginger. Whisk in the sesame oil, cover, and refrigerate.

Meanwhile, in a heatproof bowl, pour enough boiling water on the Brussels sprouts to cover. After 8 to 10 seconds, pour into a strainer and shock under cold water. Drain and blot very dry on paper towels. Return to the bowl, add the scallion, cranberries, sesame seeds, about 2 tablespoons of the vinaigrette, and black pepper to taste; toss to blend. Add more vinaigrette, if desired.

TURKISH ZUCCHINI PANCAKES WITH YOGURT-CUCUMBER SAUCE

Beyond yam and baking potato latkes (on pages 13–14), many other vegetables can be shredded and fried into tasty pancakes. On several occasions in Istanbul, I enjoyed this combination of zucchini, scallions, dill, oregano, feta, and pine nuts, known as mücver. *Lebanese cooks call zucchini fritters* ejjeh koussa. *The cacik sauce is very similar to Greek tzatziki.*

1 cup coarsely grated zucchini (about 4 ounces) by hand or in a food processor fitted with a coarse shredding disk

¼ teaspoon kosher salt or coarse sea salt, divided

Yogurt-Cucumber Sauce (page 83)

⅓ cup chopped scallions, including most of the green parts

1 large egg, beaten

1½ tablespoons chopped fresh dill or 1½ teaspoons dried dill weed

1½ tablespoons chopped fresh mint leaves or flat-leaf parsley

Freshly ground black pepper

2 tablespoons all-purpose flour

2 tablespoons crumbled feta cheese

2 tablespoons pine nuts or sunflower seeds, lightly toasted

Olive oil, for frying

In a colander or large strainer, toss the zucchini with ⅛ teaspoon of salt and drain for 25 minutes. Meanwhile, prepare the Yogurt-Cucumber Sauce and set aside.

Squeeze the zucchini with your hands to remove as much moisture as possible, transfer to a kitchen towel or several layers of paper towels, and squeeze again. In a bowl, combine the zucchini, scallions, egg, dill, mint or parsley, the remaining salt, and a generous amount of pepper; mix well. Stir in the flour and then add the feta. Before cooking, stir in the pine nuts.

If not serving right away, preheat the oven to 300°F. Line a flat dish with a paper towel and put it in the oven.

Heat an 8-inch cast-iron skillet over medium heat until hot but not smoking. Measure scant ½-cupfuls of the mixture and form into two 3-inch patties. Add enough oil to coat the bottom of the pan. When it shimmers, slide the pancakes into the pan and gently flatten slightly with the back of a spatula. Fry until golden brown, 2½ to 3 minutes per side, turning once. Serve right away with a generous dollop of the Yogurt-Cucumber Sauce or keep warm in the oven.

Yogurt-Cucumber Sauce (Cacik)

⅓ cup full-fat Greek-style plain yogurt
½ small cucumber, grated and blotted dry, or use a Persian cucumber
1 medium shallot, finely chopped
1 large clove garlic, minced
Pinch salt
1 tablespoon extra-virgin olive oil
2 tablespoons chopped fresh mint leaves

In the bowl, stir together the yogurt, cucumber, shallot, garlic, and salt. Stir in the oil. Before serving, fold in the mint.

GRILLED BELGIAN ENDIVE
WITH ANCHOVY VINAIGRETTE

I love grilled endive, as well as grilled radicchio, and even small heads of romaine. With the help of a grill pan, they acquire not only a slightly charred, earthy taste but those tempting hash marks that make them among my favorite side dishes to serve with roast chicken or grilled fish.

3 canned anchovy fillets, blotted dry
2 medium or large cloves garlic
2 tablespoons extra-virgin olive oil, plus oil to brush on the pan and endive
2 teaspoons mayonnaise
1½ teaspoons freshly squeezed lemon juice
1 teaspoon Dijon mustard
Pinch red pepper flakes
2 medium Belgian endive, trimmed and cut in half lengthwise, leaving the base intact, or a very small head of radicchio
Kosher salt or coarse sea salt
Freshly ground black pepper
Minced flat-leaf parsley, for garnish

In a mini food processor, combine the anchovy fillets, garlic, olive oil, mayonnaise, lemon juice, mustard, and pepper flakes; process until smooth.

Heat a 10-inch cast-iron grill pan over high heat until very hot but not smoking. Brush with a little oil and adjust the heat to medium-high.

Brush the endive generously with oil and season liberally with salt and pepper. Lay the halves cut-side down in the pan, reduce the heat to medium-high, and grill for a total of 5 to 6 minutes, using tongs to turn them two or three times to cook them through and create hash marks on both sides. Remove and serve with the anchovy vinaigrette spooned on top and garnished with a little parsley.

WHAT TO DO WITH EXTRA SAGE LEAVES

I first tasted fresh sage leaves in the rustic Florentine kitchen of the late Giuliano Bugialli. He had lightly battered the velvety, gray-green leaves, deep-fried them, and served them drizzled with lemon juice and coarse salt. The difference in taste between the fresh leaves and dried herb in tins was dramatic and I've been addicted ever since.

Besides roasting potatoes, the leaves can be used in many ways. For a compound butter, mix a few chopped leaves with softened butter, minced shallots, and a pinch of salt. After chilling, add dollops to grilled chicken breasts.

Sage pesto prepared like the traditional basil sauce and drizzled over veal as it roasts is another case where it's impossible to imagine using dried leaves. The smooth purée of sage and walnuts blends with the pan juices is an elegant complement to the meat. The pesto is also superb on grilled tuna.

Finally, small amounts of sage infused into cream for ice cream is a delightful surprise.

ROASTED POTATOES WITH SAGE LEAVES IN DUCK FAT

For these visually seductive, mouthwatering potatoes, the cut halves sit on sage leaves while roasting in duck fat. They become creamy on the inside and wonderfully crunchy on the bottom. Thanks to Chef Renée Marton for sharing them. So simple, so scrumptious; maybe double the recipe and call it a meal? If you saved the fat from cooking the Plum-Cherry Glazed Duck Breasts (page 154), this is an ideal place to use some of it.

2 tablespoons rendered duck fat or olive oil
8 sage leaves
4 small white, Yukon Gold, or red potatoes (about 2½ inches long), cut in half lengthwise
Kosher salt or coarse sea salt
Freshly ground black pepper

Preheat the oven to 375°F.

In an 8- or 10-inch skillet or griddle, melt the duck fat over medium heat. Place a sage leaf on the cut side of each potato. Lay them in the pan, cut-side down, and brush the skins with duck fat. Sprinkle with salt and pepper to taste and roast in the oven until the potatoes are tender when picked with a knife tip, the sage leaves are crisp, and the bottoms are golden brown, 30 to 35 minutes.

POTATO GALETTE

This crunchy potato cake is a delicious partner for roast chicken, shrimp, sliced steak, or even with a hamburger on top of it. Season the potatoes with salt as you add them to the pan to prevent them from becoming watery. Don't worry if the slices are irregular; just press them flat in the pan. A mandoline or OXO handheld slicer can be used for the potatoes, but a food processor fitted with a 2mm thin slicing disk is a safer and quicker way to keep your fingers in good shape.

1½ tablespoons extra-virgin olive oil
½ small yellow onion, thinly sliced
12 ounces small Yukon Gold or red potatoes, scrubbed
1 teaspoon minced fresh rosemary leaves
1 small clove garlic, minced
Sea salt
Freshly ground black pepper
1–2 tablespoons grated Parmigiano-Reggiano (optional)

Preheat the oven to 425°F.

Heat an 8-inch cast-iron skillet over medium-high heat until hot but not smoking. Add a little of the oil and the onion and sauté until soft and golden. Transfer to a medium-size bowl and stir in the rosemary, garlic, and 1 tablespoon of the oil.

In a food processor fitted with a 2mm slicing disk, or using a handheld slicer, slice the potatoes, transfer them to the bowl with the oil, and turn to coat evenly. Add the potato slices to the skillet in three batches, layering them in an overlapping pattern, lightly seasoning each layer with salt and pepper and a drizzle of oil.

Heat the pan over high until you hear sizzling noises. Transfer it to the middle of the oven and bake until the potatoes are tender and lightly browned on the edges, about 30 minutes. If desired, sprinkle on the cheese and run briefly under the broiler until the cheese is lightly browned. Remove, let stand a few minutes, and serve.

BREAD PUDDING WITH TUSCAN ROASTED VEGETABLES

Oven roasting is among my favorite ways to enjoy peppers, onion, and many other vegetables. I first fell in love with roasted vegetables while working in Florence. In this bread pudding, they are folded together with purchased or Quick Homemade Pesto and aged Pecorino Toscano cheese, which is more intense tasting than Parmigiano-Reggiano.

1 tablespoon extra-virgin olive oil or oil from the oil-cured tomatoes

2½–3 cups thickly sliced or diced mixed vegetables (see above)

2 cloves garlic, split

1 teaspoon dried thyme

Salt

Freshly ground black pepper

2 tablespoons Quick Homemade Pesto (page 12) or purchased pesto

1 cup whole milk, or more, depending how dry the bread is

2 large eggs

3–4 slices stale or oven dried Italian bread, torn into 1–2-inch pieces (about 4 cups loosely packed); an Italian sub sandwich roll works well

⅓ cup grated aged Pecorino Toscano cheese or other hard grating cheese

2 tablespoons finely chopped sun-dried, oil-cured tomatoes

1 tablespoon pine nuts, toasted

1 tablespoon chopped flat-leaf parsley, for garnish

Preheat the oven to 425°F. Brush an 8-inch cast-iron skillet with a little oil.

Add the cut-up vegetables, garlic, thyme, and remaining olive oil to the skillet. Season to taste with salt and pepper and turn to coat evenly. Roast in the lower third of the oven until the vegetables are wilted and lightly browned on the edges, 20 to 25 minutes, turning a few times. Remove and set aside. Adjust the heat to 350°F.

Meanwhile, prepare the Quick Homemade Pesto, if using. In a large bowl, combine the milk and eggs, with the pesto. Add the bread, turn to coat evenly, and set aside to let the liquid absorb, 10 to 15 minutes or longer, depending on how dry the bread is. If there are still dry areas in the center of the cubes, add a little more milk.

Reheat the pan over medium-high heat. Gently fold the vegetables, cheese, sun-dried tomatoes, and pine nuts into the bread; scrape into the skillet. Cover with foil and bake for 25 minutes. Uncover and bake until the top is browned and bubbling. Run briefly under the broiler for a couple minutes to brown the top, if desired. Remove, sprinkle on the parsley, let it stand for 10 minutes, and serve.

4. Seafood

Green Pozole with Clams and Fresh Tuna   95

Tempura-Fried Oysters on Baby Greens, Avocado, and Cherry Tomato Salad with Avocado Green Goddess Dressing   97

Mussels Steamed in Beer with Leeks, Bacon, and a Touch of Cream   101

Spicy Beer-Battered Shrimp with Remoulade Sauce   102

Pan-Seared Diver Scallops over Kale   105

Pan-Fried Catfish Kerala-Style with Indian Tartar Sauce   106

Oven-Roasted Shrimp, Cauliflower, and Cherry Tomatoes   109

Poached Arctic Char Provençal with Fennel Vinaigrette   111

Seared, Roasted Cod with Shiitakes, Scallions, and Grapes   112

Roasted Salmon Pastrami   114

Cornmeal-Crusted Salmon Fillets with Mango–Red Pepper Black Bean Salsa   117

Balsamic-Glazed Swordfish with Harissa Herb Butter and Coconut Kale   119

Asian Salade Niçoise with Sesame-Crusted Tuna   121

Thai Tuna Burger   125

GREEN POZOLE WITH CLAMS AND FRESH TUNA

Native Americans gave us many culinary gifts, including clambakes from New England's Penobscot tribe and pozole, this soupy-stew, from Mexico. In the Nahuatl language, the word pozole *means "hominy," the dried kernels of corn with the hulls and germ removed, that is the traditional base of this dish.*

Like cioppino and bouillabaisse, there are numerous versions of pozole, including those that are red, white, and green in color, each with different seasonings, and those with pork and chicken. Garnishes often include sliced radishes and cabbage, but diced avocado and chopped scallions are also welcome. While often served to celebrate the New Year, pozole is a perfect salve on any cold, blustery day.

4–5 ounces sushi-grade tuna, cut into ¾-inch cubes

1 teaspoon ground coriander, plus more to season the tuna

1 teaspoon ground cumin, plus more to season the tuna

Salt

¼ pound tomatillos, husked

1 chipotle in adobo

1 tablespoons olive oil, plus ½ tablespoon to cook the tuna

1 small yellow onion, peeled and finely chopped

2 large garlic cloves, finely chopped

1–1½ cups clam broth or chicken broth, depending how thick you like the pozole

1 (15-ounce) can hominy, preferably white, rinsed and drained

½ cup fresh corn kernels, defrosted frozen, or canned kernels

½ teaspoon dried oregano, preferably Mexican

8 littleneck clams, scrubbed

Freshly ground black pepper

3 tablespoons chopped fresh cilantro leaves

Lime wedges, sliced radishes, and shredded cabbage, to garnish

Season the tuna with coriander, cumin, and salt. Set aside on a plate. Bring a small pot of water to a boil, add the tomatillos, and gently boil until soft, about 8 minutes; drain, transfer to the jar of a mini food processor or electric blender with the chipotle, and purée.

Meanwhile, heat an 8- or 10-inch cast-iron skillet over medium heat until hot but not smoking. Add the oil and onion and sauté until soft, 3 to 4 minutes, stirring occasionally. Add the garlic, cumin, and coriander, and stir until fragrant, about 1 minute. Stir in the tomatillo mixture, 1 cup of broth, the hominy, corn, and oregano; cover and simmer for

(Directions continued on next page)

30 minutes. Add the clams, ½ teaspoon of salt or to taste, and plenty of pepper; cover and simmer until the clams open, about 5 minutes, adding more broth, if desired.

In a small skillet (another cast-iron skillet if you have one), heat the remaining oil over medium-high heat. Stir in the tuna cubes and cook just until lightly browned on all sides but dark pink in the center, 1 to 2 minutes, turning often. Divide the soup between two flat bowls. Add the tuna and cilantro to the bowls, and garnish with radishes, shredded cabbage, and lime quarters.

TEMPURA-FRIED OYSTERS ON BABY GREENS, AVOCADO, AND CHERRY TOMATO SALAD WITH AVOCADO GREEN GODDESS DRESSING

Rather than ho-hum croutons, consider crunchy, tempura-fried oysters as a sophisticated embellishment for this salad of tender baby greens, avocado, cherry tomatoes, and red onion with Avocado Green Goddess Dressing. Or skip the salad and put those oysters on buttered, grilled hot dog buns for a classic summertime treat.

"For frying, rice flour is a great way to use less coating than wheat flour, although it browns faster, so smaller pieces are recommended," says my friend Chef Renée Marton. "Think tempura versus fried chicken: good for crispness but not for chewiness." It also absorbs less oil. Cornstarch also helps make a crunchy coating. This batter is gluten-free. Renée's informative book Rice: A Global History *was published in 2014.*

Avocado Green Goddess Dressing (page 99)
4 cups loosely packed field greens such as baby kale, frisée, and watercress
6 grape or cherry tomatoes, halved
1 tablespoon roasted pumpkin seeds
2 tablespoons finely chopped red onion
⅓ cup rice flour
¼ cup cornstarch
Generous pinch salt
¼+ cup cold club soda
2 tablespoons finely chopped flat-leaf parsley
6–8 shucked oysters, according to taste, drained in a strainer
Canola or peanut oil
½ ripe avocado, preferably Hass variety (reserved from dressing), peeled and sliced lengthwise

Make the Avocado Green Goddess Dressing.

Divide the greens, cherry tomatoes, pumpkin seeds, and red onion between two wide, flat soup bowls or large plates.

In a medium bowl, stir together the rice flour, cornstarch, and salt. Slowly whisk in the club soda until the batter is smooth. Stir in the parsley. The batter should just coat the back of a spoon. Add a little more flour, if needed; if too thick, add a little more club soda.

Pat the oysters dry on paper towels. In a 6-inch cast-iron skillet, add enough oil to measure ¾-inch deep. Heat over medium heat until the oil measures about 360°F on an instant-read thermometer or until a

(Directions continued on page 99)

1-inch cube of bread dropped in the oil browns in a minute. If you prefer, use an 8-inch skillet, but it will take more oil.

Working in batches of 2, dip the oysters in the batter one at a time, lift out, letting any excess fall into the bowl, and carefully add to the oil. Cook until richly browned on all sides, 2 to 3 minutes, turning as needed. Transfer to paper towels to drain.

Once the oysters are cooked, add them and the avocado slices to the bowls. Spoon some of the dressing over each salad, season with salt and fresh ground pepper, if needed, and serve. Pass the remaining dressing at the table, if desired.

Avocado Green Goddess Dressing
Makes 1½ cups

In this creamy-spicy, bright green condiment, scallions, parsley, cilantro, tarragon, and jalapeño are puréed with avocado, buttermilk, and mayonnaise. It takes minutes in a food processor or electric blender and keeps for months in a sealed jar in the refrigerator. Besides being a scrumptious salad dressing, use as a dip for vegetables (both cooked and raw), other fish dishes, or as a sandwich spread.

½ cup packed flat-leaf parsley
2 scallions, including most of the green parts, coarsely chopped
1 oil-packed anchovy fillet or ½ teaspoon anchovy paste
1 large garlic clove, coarsely chopped
½ avocado, preferably Hass variety, coarsely chopped (use other half for the salad)
½ jalapeño, seeds and membranes removed, coarsely chopped

1½ tablespoons capers
1½ tablespoons fresh tarragon leaves
1 tablespoon freshly squeezed lemon juice
⅔ cup buttermilk
⅓ cup mayonnaise
Salt
Freshly ground black pepper

In a food processor, pulse the parsley, scallions, anchovy, garlic, avocado, jalapeño, capers, tarragon, and lemon juice until fairly finely chopped. Add the buttermilk and mayonnaise and process until almost smooth. Scrape into a jar and refrigerate for about 30 minutes for the flavors to develop. If the dressing is too thick, stir in a little buttermilk.

MUSSELS STEAMED IN BEER, WITH LEEKS, BACON, AND A TOUCH OF CREAM

If you and a friend adore mussels, this is an abundantly delicious way to indulge. In fewer than 20 minutes, you can dive into this generous pot of succulent mussels cooked with bacon and beer and slurp away. What a combination.

The rule of thumb for portion size is one pound of mussels per person. However, if you have smaller appetites or want to serve them as a first course or for lunch, this recipe can be divided in half, or will comfortably feed three. Garlicky toasted French bread is a must to soak up the sauce. After plucking the first mussel from the shell, use an empty shell as a pincer to remove the rest. It's fun and easy.

2 very thick slices smoky bacon, cut crosswise into ¼–½-inch lardons

1 tablespoon olive oil, or more, as needed

White and pale green parts of 1 medium leek, thinly sliced (about ½ cup)

1 tablespoon finely chopped garlic

2 tablespoons chopped flat-leaf parsley, plus additional for garnish

2 tablespoons chopped fresh thyme leaves

1 cup IPA or lager beer

¾ cup fish or chicken broth

3 tablespoons whole grain Pommery mustard

¼ cup heavy cream

Generous pinch red pepper flakes

2 pounds farmed mussels, scrubbed and debearded

Coarse sea salt

Freshly ground black pepper

½-inch-thick slices French bread, grilled or toasted, rubbed with olive oil and garlic

In a deep 10-inch cast-iron skillet or pot, combine the bacon and 1 tablespoon of the oil. Heat over medium-high heat and sauté until the bacon pieces are almost cooked through, about 4 minutes, stirring occasionally. Remove with a slotted spoon and set aside.

Add enough oil to the pan to measure about 1 tablespoon of fat. Stir in the leek and cook over medium heat until wilted, 5 minutes. Add the garlic and herbs, cook for 30 seconds, then add the mussels in a single layer. Pour in the beer and broth, cover, and cook over high heat until the mussels have opened, about 5 minutes, shaking the pan a couple times. With a slotted spoon, remove them to a large bowl and tent with foil. Discard any mussels that don't open.

Stir in the beer, broth, heavy cream, mustard, and red pepper flakes; boil until the liquid is reduced by half.

Add the mussels in a single layer, cover the pan, and cook over high heat until the mussels have opened, about 5 minutes, shaking the pan a couple times. Return the bacon to the pan to heat through, season to taste with salt and pepper, and serve the mussels garnished with the remaining herbs. Serve with the toasted or grilled bread.

SPICY BEER-BATTERED SHRIMP
WITH REMOULADE SAUCE

These seductive beer-battered shrimp dipped in tangy remoulade sauce can be a tasty appetizer for two or three or a light dinner for two. Because cast-iron pans retain the heat as more shrimp are added, the constant temperature level seals in the moisture and quickly produces perfectly cooked bites. The mayonnaise-based sauce, flavored with celery, shallot, capers, and mustard, is brightened with fresh orange juice. Extra remoulade will keep in the refrigerator for several weeks. Use it on fried oysters, softshell crabs, or as a sandwich spread.

REMOULADE SAUCE
½ cup mayonnaise
2 tablespoons minced celery
2 tablespoons minced shallot
2 tablespoons finely chopped flat-leaf parsley, plus ½ tablespoon for garnish
1 tablespoon finely chopped capers
1 tablespoon whole-grain mustard
1 small orange to yield ½ teaspoon finely grated orange zest, plus 1 teaspoon freshly squeezed orange juice
1 teaspoon Worcestershire sauce
Kosher salt or sea salt
Finely ground black pepper

SHRIMP
Peanut or canola oil, for frying
½ cup all-purpose flour
1 tablespoon Cajun seasoning
1 tablespoon granulated sugar
Kosher salt or sea salt
½ cup pale lager beer, such as Corona
2 tablespoons hot sauce, such as Frank's RedHot Original Pepper Sauce
½ cup panko
½ cup unsweetened shredded coconut
6–9 jumbo shrimp, peeled and deveined, tails intact
Chopped flat-leaf parsley, for garnish

In a small bowl, stir together the mayonnaise, celery, shallot, parsley, capers, mustard, orange juice and zest, and Worcestershire sauce; season to taste with salt and pepper and set aside.

Turn the oven to warm (150 to 200°F). Clip a deep fat/candy thermometer to the side of a 10-inch cast-iron skillet and heat for 5 minutes. Add enough oil to measure ¾-inch deep. Heat to 360°F on a deep fat thermometer. Keep the thermometer in the pan or nearby to ensure that the shrimp do not burn.

Meanwhile, in a medium-sized bowl, combine the flour, Cajun seasoning, sugar, and ½ teaspoon of salt; slowly whisk in the beer and hot sauce to make a smooth batter. In a shallow bowl, combine the panko with the coconut.

Holding each shrimp by its tail, dip it into the batter, letting the excess fall into the bowl, then dredge it in the panko-coconut mixture, pressing and rolling it several times to cover well. Repeat with the remaining shrimp.

Add the shrimp, a few at a time, to the hot oil and fry until golden brown, about 2 minutes, turning once with tongs, adjusting the heat to keep the temperature at 360°F. Remove the shrimp with a slotted spoon to a plate lined with paper towels. Serve with remoulade sauce and a little parsley to garnish on top.

PAN-SEARED DIVER SCALLOPS OVER KALE

While driving through Nova Scotia's Annapolis Valley, I stopped for dinner at Domaine de Grand Pré, the oldest farm winery in Atlantic Canada. Jason Lynch, the executive chef of their restaurant, Le Caveau, prepared large sea scallops in a white wine and cream sauce with a hint of Pernod. It was one of the nicest scallop dishes I'd ever tasted.

Fishing trawlers have been a mainstay in the Bay of Fundy, where local Digby scallops are still highly prized. Although not available outside Canada, if you buy "dry" scallops from a reputable fishmonger and don't move them when cooking them in the pan until ready to turn, your scallops will be done perfectly. Lacinato, also called Tuscan or dinosaur kale, has become more readily available in recent years. It has a less assertive taste than common kale with intriguing textured leaves.

1 tablespoon unsalted butter
2 tablespoons minced shallots
½ cup dry white wine
¼ cup heavy cream
2 teaspoons chopped chives
1 teaspoon Pernod (optional)
8 large sea scallops, preferably
   Diver scallops, side muscle
   removed, blotted dry
Sea salt
Freshly ground black pepper
1 (6-ounce) bunch kale, preferably
   lacinato or Tuscan kale, coarse
   stems removed, cut crosswise
   into chiffonade

To easily remove coarse stems from leafy greens like kale

Grab the leaf on either side of the stem at the base and slide your fingers down the stem.

In a small saucepan over medium heat, melt ½ tablespoon of the butter. Add the shallots and sauté for 3 minutes. Pour in the wine and boil until reduced by half, about 2 minutes. Add the cream, half of the chives, and the Pernod, if using. Simmer briefly until the sauce coats the back of a spoon. Season with salt and pepper and set aside.

Heat a 10-inch cast-iron skillet over medium-high heat until hot but not smoking. Season the scallops with salt and pepper. Add the remaining butter to the pan and sauté the scallops until brown and almost cooked through, about 2 minutes per side. Don't move them while cooking. Transfer to a small plate and tent with foil to keep warm.

Add the kale to the drippings in the skillet and toss over medium-high heat until wilted, about 3 minutes. Divide the kale between two plates and place the scallops on top. Spoon on the sauce, sprinkle on the remaining chives, and serve.

PAN-FRIED CATFISH KERALA-STYLE WITH INDIAN TARTAR SAUCE

Many people think of catfish fried in cast iron as the epitome of Southern comfort food. Yet, the appeal has a global reach, as my friend May Fridel, from Kerala, showed me. She's from a long line of spice merchants, and her Indian spin on this classic is tasty and colorful.

The pieces of fish are briefly marinated in buttermilk and a spice masala, then dusted with rice flour, and quickly fried. The results are crunchy and golden on the outside yet tender inside. Serve them with Indian Tartar Sauce or chutney of your choice. Sautéed greens like sautéed broccoli rabe or kale (including the coconut kale served with the Balsamic Glazed Swordfish on page 119) make an appealing side dish.

Indian Tartar Sauce (page 107)
½ tablespoon smoked paprika
1 teaspoon ground black pepper
1 teaspoon kosher salt or sea salt
½ teaspoon ground turmeric
¼ teaspoon cayenne
1 teaspoon grated fresh garlic
1 teaspoon grated ginger
1 tablespoon freshly squeezed lemon juice, zest of ½ lemon, plus wedges to garnish
1–1½ tablespoons buttermilk
1 teaspoon sea salt, divided
10–12 ounces skinless catfish fillets, cut into 3-inch pieces
⅓ cup rice flour
1½ tablespoons coconut or canola oil, for frying
Julienned mint leaves, for garnish

Make the Indian Tartar Sauce, if using.

In a small bowl, combine the paprika, black pepper, salt, turmeric, and cayenne. Stir in the garlic, ginger, lemon juice, and lemon zest. Stir in just enough buttermilk to make a masala paste and rub onto the fish. Place on a rack and let marinate for 10 to 15 minutes.

Meanwhile, line a plate with paper towels. Heat a 10-inch cast-iron skillet over medium-high heat until hot but not smoking. Add the oil. When it shimmers, dust the catfish pieces with rice flour, patting to remove any extra, and lay them in the skillet. Cook 1 minute, turn the heat down to medium, and cook until golden brown, about 2½ to 3 minutes, watching that the pieces don't burn; turn and cook the second sides for the same amount of time.

Drain on paper towels and serve garnished with mint leaves, lemon wedges, and Indian Tartar Sauce or chutney of choice.

Indian Tartar Sauce

Makes ½ cup

⅓ cup mayonnaise
3 tablespoons minced shallots
2 tablespoons minced cilantro leaves
1 tablespoon minced gherkins or dill pickles

½ teaspoon Madras curry powder, or to taste
1 teaspoon freshly squeezed lemon juice
Red pepper flakes, if desired

In a small bowl, stir all of the ingredients together.

OVEN-ROASTED SHRIMP, CAULIFLOWER, AND CHERRY TOMATOES

An oh-so-tasty and satisfying lunch or dinner that can be served hot from the oven or at room temperature. As the mixture roasts, the cauliflower and onions become slightly charred and add an earthy taste to the flavor of the sweet shrimp and tomatoes. Grated Parmigiano-Reggiano adds a rich, nutty accent. It's a perfect one-dish meal that everyone will enjoy and can easily be doubled to serve four.

3–4 cups cauliflower florets

2 cups sliced onion

3 cloves garlic, split in half

Leaves from 3 sprigs thyme or 1 teaspoon dried leaves

½ teaspoon kosher salt or coarse sea salt, or to taste

Freshly ground black pepper to taste

Pinch red pepper flakes (optional)

2 tablespoons extra-virgin olive oil

6–8 ounces peeled and deveined large shrimp

10 cherry or grape tomatoes, halved

⅓ cup grated Parmigiano-Reggiano

Chopped flat-leaf parsley, to garnish

Put a 10-inch cast-iron skillet in the oven and preheat to 425°F.

In a large bowl, stir the cauliflower, onion, garlic, thyme, salt, pepper, and red pepper flakes, if using, together with the olive oil to coat evenly. Scrape into the skillet and return to the middle of the oven. Roast until the florets are lightly browned and almost tender, about 25 minutes, turning occasionally.

Add the shrimp and tomatoes and continue cooking until the shrimp are pink, about 12 minutes, turning once or twice. Sprinkle with the cheese and broil briefly to brown. Sprinkle with the parsley and serve.

POACHED ARCTIC CHAR PROVENÇAL WITH FENNEL VINAIGRETTE

Arctic char (also called steelhead trout) fillets have a lovely coral color and a flavor that's a cross between trout and salmon. It partners well with the tastes of Provence like fennel, olives, and capers. It was inspired by a dish served to me at the Imperial Hotel in Vienna, where I was writing about new Austrian cuisine. I guess the chef liked Provence as much as I do.

1 plum tomato, peeled, seeded, and finely chopped (about ¾ cup)

2 tablespoons coarsely chopped oil-cured black olives

1 tablespoon small capers

1½ tablespoons extra-virgin olive oil, or more if needed, divided

1 teaspoon good-quality balsamic vinegar

1 cup fennel cut into matchsticks or thin slices, some fronds reserved and chopped

1 small shallot, chopped

1 large clove garlic, chopped

¼ cup dry white wine mixed with ¼ cup fish broth or water

2 (5–6 ounces each) Arctic char fillets with skin on, blotted dry, pinbones removed

½ teaspoon dried basil

Kosher salt or coarse sea salt

Freshly ground black pepper

2 tablespoons finely chopped flat-leaf parsley

Preheat the oven to 350°F.

In a small bowl, mix together the tomato, olives, and capers with 1 tablespoon of olive oil and the balsamic vinegar. Set aside

Heat an 8-inch cast-iron skillet over medium-high heat until hot but not smoking. Add ½ teaspoon of olive oil, the fennel, and shallot. Reduce the heat to medium and sauté until lightly colored, 3½ to 4 minutes, stirring often. Add the garlic, cook for 30 seconds, then pour in the wine mixture and bring to a simmer.

Lay the fish fillets, skin-side down, in the pan. Season with basil and salt and pepper, partially cover with a lid or foil, transfer to the oven, and poach until the flesh is just opaque and feels firm to the touch, 8 to 10 minutes. Reduce the heat if the liquid boils. Transfer to two large, flat soup bowls or dinner plates and tent with foil.

Stir the reserved olive-caper mixture and parsley into the pan, bring to a boil for 5 minutes to reduce slightly, and taste to adjust the seasonings, adding ½ teaspoon more olive oil and a few drops of balsamic vinegar, if desired. Spoon the mixture over the fish, add a few fennel fronds, and serve.

SEARED, ROASTED COD WITH SHIITAKES, SCALLIONS, AND GRAPES

One day I wanted to buy halibut, but it was so expensive I opted for cod, a fish I often considered boring. Aside from its reasonable price, however, I discovered that it can be successfully cooked in many ways, especially if you buy fish that hasn't been frozen so it's less likely to fall apart. In this dressed-up but easy recipe, once the flesh side is seared on the stovetop, the fillets are turned and oven-roasted into a beautifully moist, flavorful piece of fish.

The mild taste takes well to diverse flavors. This version includes shiitake mushrooms and grapes in a light wine sauce with a touch of cream and chopped gherkins for a tangy flavor accent. A simpler way is to prepare it is with purchased or Quick Homemade Pesto (page 12) brushed on the flesh once it's seared and in the oven. Cod is also good source of omega-3 fatty acids, another plus. Serve with orzo or small boiled potatoes.

3 tablespoons extra-virgin olive oil, divided

4 ounces shiitake mushrooms, stems removed, wiped, and cut into ½-inch slices

¼ cup finely chopped scallion, mostly white parts, plus thin slices, for garnish

1 teaspoon fresh thyme leaves

¼ cup dry white wine

Salt

Freshly ground black pepper

2 thick (5–6 ounces each) skinless cod fillets, blotted dry with paper towels

¾ cup panko

⅓ cup seedless green or red grapes, cut in half or sliced, if very large

2 tablespoons heavy or light cream

1–1½ tablespoons minced gherkins or very small capers

Preheat the oven to 425°F.

Heat a 10-inch cast-iron skillet over medium-high until hot but not smoking. Add 2 tablespoons of the oil and the mushrooms, and sauté until browned, about 4 minutes, stirring often. Stir in the scallion and thyme and cook for 30 seconds. Pour in the wine, cook for 1 minute, stirring up any browned cooking bits, and season to taste with salt and pepper. Scrape into a bowl and set aside.

Wipe out the skillet, add the remaining oil, and heat until shimmering. Season the cod generously with salt and pepper, pat firmly with panko, and lay the fillets in the pan, flesh-side down, to sear until nicely browned, about 2 minutes. Do not move until ready to turn. Using a slotted spatula, carefully check the bottom of one fillet. If not browned enough, cook 1 minute more.

Turn the cod and transfer the pan to the oven. Roast until the flesh is just flaking and opaque when the tip of a knife is inserted in the middle, 5 to 6 minutes, depending on the thickness.

Transfer to two plates and tent with foil. Return the mushrooms to the pan, add the grapes, and warm over medium heat. Stir in the cream and 1 tablespoon of the gherkins. Taste to adjust the seasonings, adding the remaining gherkins if desired, and spoon the mixture over the fish. Garnish with a few sliced scallions.

ROASTED SALMON PASTRAMI

Salmon shines in Chef Kathleen Kenny Sanderson's tasty and inventive pastrami that is easy to make and delicious. Serve it as an open-faced sandwich, as hors d'oeuvres, or even for brunch. After briefly marinating, it's rubbed with ground spices and roasted in the oven.

When I started the Cookingstudio, the cooking school I founded in Kings Super Market, in New Jersey, we featured an ongoing series of "Principles" to teach all aspects of cooking. Kathleen was one of the four original instructors. We've remained friends for decades, and she's now a consultant for major food companies.

2 tablespoons soy sauce
2 tablespoons granulated sugar
2 tablespoons kosher salt
6–8 ounces center-cut salmon fillet, skinned
1 tablespoon mustard seeds
½ tablespoon coriander seeds
½ tablespoon dill seeds
¼ tablespoon cracked black pepper
2 tablespoons firmly packed dark brown sugar
1 teaspoon kosher salt or coarse sea salt
Oil, to brush in the pan
½ tablespoon prepared white horseradish
⅓ cup sour cream
Sliced pumpernickel or black bread

In a resealable plastic bag or stainless steel bowl, combine the soy sauce, sugar, and salt and mix well. Add the salmon and turn to coat evenly. Cover or seal and refrigerate for 35 to 40 minutes, turning once or twice.

Meanwhile, preheat the oven to 400°F. Heat an 8-inch cast-iron skillet over medium-high heat until hot but not smoking. Add the mustard, coriander, and dill seeds along with the pepper and toast until fragrant and the seeds begin to pop, 1 to 2 minutes, shaking the pan a couple times. Scrape into a clean coffee grinder or mortar and pestle and coarsely grind; mix with the brown sugar and salt.

Drain the salmon, rinse, and pat dry with paper towels. Heat the skillet over medium-high heat until hot but not smoking. Brush with oil.

Rub the spice mixture liberally into both sides of the salmon, lay it in the skillet, skin-side down, transfer to the oven, and roast until the flesh is just firm to the touch, 10 to 12 minutes. Cool completely in the pan, transfer to a covered container, and refrigerate.

In a small bowl, stir the horseradish into the sour cream. Bring the salmon back to room temperature. Serve it in bite-sized pieces with black bread topped with the horseradish–sour cream mixture.

CORNMEAL-CRUSTED SALMON FILLETS WITH MANGO–RED PEPPER BLACK BEAN SALSA

This simple grilled salmon dish offers a feast of colors, bold tastes, and textures. Toothsome, chili-spiced cornmeal on the surface coats the fish and keeps it succulent. Mango–Red Pepper Salsa adds a bright taste and a bold color accent to the sweet salmon. Serve with a tossed green salad and corn on the cob, if desired.

Mango–Red Pepper Salsa (page 55)
½ cup canned black beans, rinsed
 and drained
½ cup medium yellow cornmeal
 (I prefer Bob's Red Mill)
1½ teaspoons chili powder
Kosher salt or sea salt
Freshly ground black pepper
2 (6–7 ounces each) salmon fillets
 with skin on, blotted dry
Canola or other vegetable oil, to
 brush the pan
Coarsely chopped fresh cilantro
 leaves, for garnish

In a small bowl, prepare the Mango–Red Pepper Salsa, add the black beans, and set aside.

In a flat dish, combine the cornmeal, chili powder, salt, and pepper. Brush the flesh side of the salmon with a little oil. Press it (not the sides or skin) into the mixture to coat well.

Heat a 10-inch cast-iron grill pan over medium-high heat until hot but not smoking. Brush with a little oil, add the coated side of the salmon to the pan, and grill for 5 to 7 minutes, turning once about 90 degrees to create perpendicular hash marks. Turn the fish over and cook the skin side for 2 to 3 minutes. Serve on individual plates with a generous amount of salsa on top and a few cilantro leaves to garnish.

BALSAMIC-GLAZED SWORDFISH WITH HARISSA HERB BUTTER OVER COCONUT KALE

I love the "meatiness" of swordfish but think it needs a flavor boost. Here the fish is briefly marinated in balsamic glaze (available at most markets), lime juice, and olive oil before it's cooked in a grill pan or skillet. The final dollop of harissa-herb butter melts seductively over the fish and blends with the sautéed kale, pine nuts, currants, and coconut milk.

HARISSA-HERB BUTTER
2 tablespoons unsalted butter, softened
½–1 teaspoon harissa paste
1 large scallion, finely chopped and divided
Kosher salt or coarse sea salt

SWORDFISH
1 tablespoon balsamic glaze
2 teaspoons freshly squeezed lime juice
1 teaspoon extra-virgin olive oil, plus oil to brush on the pan
2 (5–6 ounces each) 1-inch-thick slices center-cut swordfish steak
Kosher salt or sea salt
Freshly ground black pepper

COCONUT KALE
1 small (about 6 ounces) bunch kale, preferably lacinato
1 tablespoon canola or other vegetable oil, divided
Salt
Freshly ground black pepper
Aleppo or cayenne pepper
1 clove garlic, minced
½ cup canned coconut milk
2 tablespoons dried currants
2 tablespoons toasted pine nuts

In a small bowl, stir together the butter, harissa paste, 1 teaspoon of the chopped scallion (reserve the remainder for the kale), and ⅛ teaspoon of salt until blended. Cover and chill until ready to serve.

Start heating a 10-inch cast-iron grill pan or skillet over medium-high heat until very hot.

In a small bowl, combine the balsamic glaze, lime juice, and oil. Brush it over the fish, turning to coat, and season both sides generously with salt and pepper. Set aside.

Meanwhile, wash the kale and shake dry, leaving excess water on the leaves. Remove the thick stems and coarsely chop the leaves. In an 8-inch skillet, heat 2 teaspoons of the oil over medium-high heat until hot but not smoking. Add the kale and sauté until wilted, 2 to 3 minutes, turning often with tongs. Remove to a bowl, season with salt, pepper, and a pinch of Aleppo or cayenne pepper.

(Directions continued on next page)

Add the remaining oil to the skillet, if needed, along with the remaining scallion and garlic; sauté until wilted, 1 minute. Return the kale to the pan. Stir in the coconut milk and cook over medium-high heat until the liquid is reduced and coats the kale. Stir in the currants, and pine nuts, and taste to adjust the seasonings. Keep warm.

Brush the hot grill pan with oil. Place the swordfish in the pan, brush with a little marinade, and cook for 2½ to 3 minutes; using tongs, turn the steaks over, brush the second side with the glaze, and cook again for 2½ to 3 minutes. Turn it back over, brush again, placing the pieces perpendicular to where they were before; and cook for 1½ to 2 minutes, creating hash marks. Finally, repeat on the second side.

Divide the kale between two dinner plates. Place the swordfish on the kale, add a generous dollop of the harissa herb butter on top of the fish, and serve.

ASIAN SALADE NIÇOISE
WITH SESAME-CRUSTED TUNA

Black and white sesame seeds add a dramatic touch to grilled sushi-grade tuna in this Asian variation on salade Niçoise. Serve it for lunch or a light dinner. If you like to change or embellish recipes as I frequently do, you might add snow peas or sugar snaps, Asian greens like tatsoi, and daikon radish cubes. The vinaigrette can be prepared several days ahead of time and refrigerated.

Orange-Sesame Vinaigrette
  (page 122) or purchased Asian
  vinaigrette

SALAD
2 small potatoes, preferably Yukon
  Gold
Kosher salt or sea salt
3–4 ounces thin green beans,
  stringed, if needed
4 cups (2 ounces) mixed field greens
2 large eggs, hard-cooked, peeled,
  and quartered

TUNA
4 tablespoons black sesame seeds
4 tablespoons white sesame seeds
Vegetable oil to brush on the tuna
  and the pan
2 (3½–4 ounces each) sushi-grade
  tuna steaks, 1 inch thick, blotted
  dry
Salt
Freshly ground black pepper
1 large scallion, including most of
  green part, thinly sliced on the
  diagonal
¼ cup finely diced red bell pepper
1 tablespoon julienned mint
  leaves, for garnish

Make the Orange-Sesame Vinaigrette, if using.

In a small saucepan, combine the potatoes, some salt, and enough cold water to cover them by an inch and bring to a boil. Cover, reduce the heat to medium-low, and gently boil until the potatoes are just tender when the tip of a knife is inserted, 6 to 8 minutes, depending on the size. Remove with a slotted spoon, cool, peel, and slice. In the same saucepan, boil the green beans until crisp-tender, rinse under cold water, and blot dry.

Divide the green beans, potatoes, and hard cooked eggs between two large, flat soup bowls or dinner plates.

In a flat dish, combine the sesame seeds. Brush the tuna with a little oil, season generously with salt and pepper, and press them into the sesame seeds, turning to cover all sides.

Heat an 8- or 10-inch cast-iron skillet over medium-high heat until hot but not smoking. Brush with a little oil, add the tuna, and cook for 1 to 2 minutes on the first side without moving, for almost rare to

(Directions continued on next page)

medium-rare or barely pink. Using a spatula, turn the tuna and cook the second side for the same amount of time. Remove and let stand for about 5 minutes. Cut across the grain into ½-inch-thick slices and lay them in the center of each plate. Sprinkle with the scallions and red pepper. Spoon some of the dressing over the salad, sprinkle with the mint, and serve. Pass the extra vinaigrette at the table.

ORANGE-SESAME ASIAN VINAIGRETTE
Yields ½ cup (*Use extra for Thai Tuna Burgers.*)

1-inch piece fresh ginger root, coarsely chopped, or 2 tablespoons finely chopped fresh ginger root
1 tablespoon lemongrass paste or 1 stalk lemongrass, trimmed and tender center finely chopped
1 large clove garlic, split
¼ cup toasted sesame oil
3 tablespoons freshly squeezed orange juice
2 tablespoons seasoned rice vinegar
½ teaspoon soy sauce
Pinch red pepper flakes

In a mini food processor, combine the ginger, lemongrass paste, and garlic and purée. Add the sesame oil, orange juice, rice vinegar, soy sauce, and pepper flakes and process until smooth. Scrape into a small bowl, cover, and refrigerate while preparing the salad and tuna, or prepare a day before. Before serving, pour the vinaigrette through a fine strainer, pressing to extract as much liquid as possible.

THAI TUNA BURGER

In this Thai-inspired burger, a little mayonnaise mixed with sriracha binds the tiny cubes of tuna and infuses the tastes of ginger, red onion, and cilantro throughout. The trick to preparing juicy burgers—including tuna, beef, and turkey—is to gently mix them just until blended. Don't press on them while cooking because it squeezes out the juices and flavor. When cutting the tuna into small cubes, it will be easier if the fish is well chilled.

From there, build the burger with your choice of condiments and bun. Bread and butter pickles, Pickled Red Onions (page 55), sweet Thai chili sauce, or a thinly sliced Persian cucumber tossed with Asian vinaigrette (below), are all great additions.

Orange-Sesame Asian Vinaigrette (page 122) or purchased Asian dressing

6–7 ounces well-chilled sushi-grade tuna, cut into ¼-inch cubes

2½ tablespoons minced red onion, divided

1½ tablespoon finely chopped cilantro leaves, divided, plus 1 teaspoon for mayonnaise topping

2 tablespoons mayonnaise, divided, plus 1 tablespoon for mayonnaise topping

2 teaspoons finely grated fresh ginger root

1 teaspoon toasted sesame oil

1 teaspoon Thai fish sauce

⅛–¼ teaspoon sriracha sauce, or to taste

Kosher salt or sea salt

Freshly ground black pepper

1 Persian cucumber, thinly sliced

1 teaspoon roasted hulled sesame seeds

1 teaspoon Thai sweet chili sauce

Canola or other vegetable oil, to brush on the pan

2 brioche hamburger buns or kaiser rolls, lightly grilled or toasted

2 romaine lettuce leaves

Make the Orange-Sesame Asian Vinaigrette, if using.

In a medium bowl, gently toss the tuna, 2 tablespoons of red onion, 1 tablespoon of cilantro, 1 tablespoon of mayonnaise, the ginger, sesame oil, and sriracha together. Season to taste with salt and pepper; shape into 2 patties about 1 inch thick, put on a plate, cover, and chill for at least 30 minutes, or a couple hours.

In a small bowl, stir together the cucumber, sesame seeds, remaining red onion and cilantro with enough Asian Vinaigrette to lightly coat. Season to taste with salt and pepper. In another small bowl, stir the remaining mayonnaise and Thai sweet chili sauce together.

Preheat a 10-inch cast-iron grill pan or skillet over medium heat until hot but not smoking. Brush with oil, add the burgers, and cook 1½ to 2 minutes per side, turning once for medium-rare, or to your liking. With a spatula, transfer the burgers onto the bun bottoms. Add a lettuce leaf and some Persian cucumbers, a spoonful of the Thai chili mayonnaise, and the bun tops.

5. Poultry

INDIAN TEA-SPICED CHICKEN BREASTS WITH GREEN CHUTNEY

In India, clay ovens called "tandoors" are used for foods traditionally marinated in yogurt and spices and then cooked over very high heat. The results are highly flavorful and juicy. While I don't have a tandoor, this chicken imitates the flavors. Indian spiced tea (chai) mixed with the yogurt and other seasonings tenderizes the breasts and imparts a delicate flavor. Serve the breasts warm or room temperature with purchased or homemade Green Chutney, basmati rice, and wedges of lemons.

Tea is a wonderfully versatile addition to all kinds of foods. It adds color, texture, and taste, for example. For decades, I've had the pleasure of working with Harney & Sons Teas and wrote two books about cooking with tea with the company's founder, the late John Harney.

2 large bone-in chicken breasts with skin on
2 sachets Indian spice tea leaves (I use Harney & Sons cinnamon-spice)
1 small onion, coarsely chopped
1 clove garlic
½ cup plain yogurt (not Greek style), regular or lowfat
1 tablespoon freshly squeezed lemon juice
1 tablespoon coarsely chopped fresh ginger root
1 teaspoon smoked paprika
½ teaspoon salt or more to taste
Freshly ground black pepper
⅛ teaspoon red pepper flakes
Green Chutney (page 130) or purchased mint green chutney
½ tablespoon ghee (clarified butter) or canola oil
Lemon wedges, to garnish
Naan bread

Using poultry shears, cut off any excess rib meat, bones, and fat.

In a spice mill, clean coffee grinder or mortar and pestle, finely grind the tea leaves, and transfer them to an electric blender. Add the onion, garlic, yogurt, lemon juice, ginger, paprika, salt, black pepper, and red pepper flakes; purée until smooth, scraping down the sides a couple of times.

Scrape the mixture into a resealable plastic bag or small glass container, add the breasts, and turn to coat evenly. Seal and refrigerate for at least 8 hours or overnight, turning once or twice.

Make the Green Chutney.

Place an 8-inch cast-iron skillet in the oven and preheat to 350°F.

(Directions continued on next page)

Remove the breasts from the plastic bag, scrape off the marinade, blot the skin side very dry with paper towels, and season with salt and pepper to taste. Reserve the marinade.

Carefully remove the skillet from the oven and place over medium-high heat on top of the stove. Add the ghee or oil and the breasts, skin-side down, and cook until the skin is crisp and golden, about 5 minutes. Turn them over, spoon a thin layer of the remaining marinade over the skin, return to the oven, and bake until the breasts are just cooked through and an instant-read thermometer reads close to 165°F, 15 to 17 minutes, or longer, depending on size and how thick they are. Remove the meat in one piece from the bones, return to the skillet flesh-side down, and cook on top of the stove over medium-high heat for 1 to 2 minutes or until done.

Transfer to a warm platter, tent with foil, and let rest for 10 minutes. Serve warm or at room temperature with Green Chutney on top, along with lemon wedges and naan, if desired.

Green Chutney

2 cups mixed cilantro and mint leaves
1 medium-small jalapeño, seeds and membranes removed, if you prefer it less spicy
1-inch piece fresh ginger root, chopped
1 large clove garlic
½ tablespoon freshly squeezed orange or lemon juice
¼–½ teaspoon sugar
⅛ teaspoon salt
2–4 tablespoons water, or enough to make the chutney smooth but not runny

In an electric blender, combine all of the ingredients and purée until completely smooth. Scrape into a bowl.

MOROCCAN CHICKEN BREASTS WITH CAULIFLOWER, GREEN OLIVES, AND POMEGRANATE SEEDS

I find chicken thighs are juicier and more flavorful than breasts, but in this combination of diced white meat, cauliflower, and green olives braised in a mildly spicy, lemon-scented sauce, and topped with pomegranate seeds, the chicken is very succulent. The dish was inspired by some aromatic tagines in Morocco and is as colorful as that sun-drenched country.

While the flavors suggest ancient Fez or Marrakesh, two convenience items make the cooking faster and easier. Pure lemon paste with a little salt added is a good stand-in for preserved lemons' briny-citrus taste, and purchased ras el hanout, a spice blend traditionally made with 8 or 10 herbs and spices, is far more efficient. Each spice merchant makes his signature blend, and the name means "top of the shop" in Arabic. To my taste, the jar I bought locally needed a little more smoked paprika and turmeric to reflect the flavors I recall in Fez, but tweak the seasonings to please your palate.

Buy green Castelveltrano olives or, as Paula Wolfert suggests, canned green olives that she says most closely approximate the texture of those in Morocco. Serve over couscous, if desired.

---

1 tablespoon all-purpose flour
2 teaspoons *ras el hanout*
¼ teaspoon smoked paprika
⅛ teaspoon ground turmeric
8 ounces boneless skinless chicken breasts, cut into 1½-inch cubes
2 tablespoons extra-virgin olive oil, divided
Kosher salt or coarse sea salt
Freshly ground black pepper
1 small onion, chopped
1 large clove garlic, minced

1 cup chicken broth
Generous pinch saffron threads crumbled and dissolved in a little warm water
1 teaspoon lemon paste (I use Nielsen-Massey)
1 cup small cauliflower florets
½ cup coarsely chopped pitted green olives (see headnote above)
3 tablespoons coarsely chopped flat-leaf parsley
½ cup pomegranate seeds
Cooked couscous to serve with the chicken, if desired

Heat an 8-inch cast-iron skillet over medium-high heat until hot but not smoking. Meanwhile, in a bowl, combine the flour, *ras el hanout*, paprika, and turmeric; add the chicken pieces and toss to coat evenly. Pat to remove any excess.

(Directions continued on page 132)

Pour 1 tablespoon of oil into the hot skillet. When shimmering, quickly brown half the chicken pieces on all sides, about 2 minutes. Using a slotted spoon, remove to a bowl and repeat with the remaining pieces. Season liberally with salt and pepper and set aside.

Add the remaining oil, the extra seasonings left in the bowl, and the onion to the skillet, and sauté 2 to 3 minutes until the onion is golden. Add the garlic, cook for 30 seconds, and stir in the broth, saffron, and lemon paste. Add the cauliflower, bring to a boil, reduce the heat to low, partially cover, and simmer until the cauliflower is almost tender, about 8 minutes. Return the chicken to the pan and gently simmer until it is just cooked through, about 5 to 6 minutes. Stir in the olives and parsley, sprinkle with the pomegranate seeds, and serve over couscous, if desired.

CURRIED CHICKEN AND WILD MUSHROOM POTPIE

Years ago, I wrote an article about potpies for the Washington Post. *One recipe was a wild mushroom ragout topped with puff pastry created by Chef Jeff Tomchek, formerly the co-owner and executive chef of Indigo restaurant, in Great Falls, Virginia. His clever method of baking the top crust separately results in a golden dome with not a bit of sogginess. I lifted his lid idea for this recipe.*

Serve with basmati rice and mango chutney, if desired. Use remaining puff pastry for other potpies. Jeff Tomchek is currently the chef-owner of 201 Restaurant, in Highwood, Illinois.

---

1 (14-ounce) package all-butter puff pastry, defrosted according to package directions (I prefer Dufour Kitchens)
1 egg mixed with a little water, to glaze the pastry
½ cup pearl onions, or use frozen pearl onions
1½ tablespoons unsalted butter
2 tablespoons all-purpose flour
¼ cup chicken broth
2 tablespoons medium sherry, plus a little more, if needed
¼ cup milk or light cream
1 tablespoon freshly squeezed lemon juice

½ tablespoon grated or finely chopped fresh ginger root
1 clove garlic, finely chopped
½ tablespoon hot or mild curry powder
Pinch cayenne
Kosher salt or sea salt
Freshly ground black pepper
8–9 ounces boneless skinless chicken breasts or thighs, well trimmed and cut into large cubes
⅓ cup diced carrots, blanched for 2 minutes
⅓ cup defrosted frozen petites peas
2 ounces shiitake or other wild mushrooms, stemmed, wiped, trimmed, and sliced
1½ tablespoons chopped flat-leaf parsley

Preheat the oven to 375°F. Line a cookie sheet with parchment paper or a Silpat.

On a lightly floured counter, unfold the dough and cut off about an 8-inch square from the sheet; roll it out to a thickness of ⅛ inch, dusting with flour occasionally. Wrap and chill the remainders. Using a sharp knife and an 8-inch plate or other form, cut out a circle, chill in the refrigerator for 15 minutes, then transfer it to the prepared cookie sheet, lightly brush with the egg wash, and bake until richly browned, about 30 minutes. Remove and set on a rack to cool.

If using fresh pearl onions, pare a thin slice from the root ends and cut a shallow "X" into them. In a small saucepan, liberally cover the onions with water, bring to a boil, and cook

(Directions continued on next page)

for 2 minutes. Drain, and when cool enough to handle, gently squeeze with your fingers to slip off the skins.

Meanwhile, in an 8-inch cast-iron skillet, melt the butter over medium-high heat until hot but not smoking. When it foams, whisk in the flour, adjust the heat to medium-low, and cook until the flour is a light cream color, about 2 minutes. Stir in the broth, sherry, milk, and lemon juice; turn the heat to medium-high and bring to a boil, stirring constantly. Cook for 30 seconds. The mixture will be quite thick.

Remove from the heat, stir in the ginger, garlic, curry, cayenne, salt, and pepper. Let the mixture cool slightly, and then fold in the chicken, onions, carrots, peas, mushrooms, and parsley.

Partially cover the pan with a lid or foil, transfer it to the oven, and bake until the chicken is just cooked though, about 18 minutes, stirring once or twice. Stir in a little sherry or broth if the sauce is too dry. Carefully place the puff pastry on top, return to the oven briefly to warm, if needed, and serve with mango chutney and basmati rice, if desired.

SICILIAN BAKED CHICKEN WITH GREEN OLIVES, GOLDEN RAISINS, CAPERS, AND PINE NUTS

Moorish, Greek, and Italian influences are woven together in this robust baked chicken with Sicilian caponata. The tastes of sweet and tangy raisins and oranges dance with salty olives and capers in the topping that's spooned over the crunchy thighs. Make the topping ahead, if you prefer, and gently reheat before serving. This makes a generous amount of caponata so you could cook a third thigh, but I suggest tossing it with fettuccine noodles as a base for the chicken.

CAPONATA TOPPING

2 tablespoons extra-virgin olive oil, divided

1 medium onion, thinly sliced crosswise

1 medium rib celery, cut into ½-inch dice

1 large clove garlic, minced

⅓ cup dry white wine diluted with ⅓ cup water

⅓ cup golden raisins

¼ cup sliced Sicilian-style green olives

1 tablespoon tomato paste

1 tablespoon small capers, drained

¼ cup oil-cured sun-dried tomatoes, chopped

2 (2-inch x ½-inch) strips orange zest, plus orange segments for the final garnish

Salt

Freshly ground black pepper

Place a 10-inch cast-iron skillet in the oven and preheat to 350°F.

In a medium-sized nonreactive skillet, heat 1½ tablespoons of the oil over medium-high heat until hot but not smoking. Add the onion, separating the pieces into rings, adjust the heat to medium-low, and sauté until the onion is wilted, about 3 minutes, stirring occasionally. Add the celery and garlic and continue cooking until the onion is golden, 5 to 6 minutes.

Pour in the wine, and bring to a boil over high heat, stirring up any browned bits. Add the raisins, olives, tomato paste, and capers. Lower the heat so the liquid gently boils, and reduce until almost evaporated, 12 to 15 minutes. Stir in the sun-dried tomatoes, orange zest, salt to taste, and a liberal amount of black pepper. Cover and keep warm while cooking the chicken.

(Ingredients and Directions continued on next page)

CHICKEN

½ cup fresh bread crumbs
Kosher salt or sea salt
Freshly ground black pepper
½ teaspoon dried thyme leaves
2 large bone-in chicken thighs,
   excess fat and skin trimmed,
   blotted dry
2 tablespoons pine nuts, lightly
   toasted
2 tablespoons chopped mint and
   mint sprigs, to garnish
Cooked fettuccine noodles to
   serve with the chicken, if
   desired

Meanwhile, in a flat dish, season the bread crumbs with salt and pepper to taste and add the thyme. Coat the chicken pieces with the crumbs, patting to cover all sides. Remove the skillet from the oven and brush with the remaining oil. Add the thighs, flesh-side down, reduce the heat to medium, and cook until the skin is crisp and richly browned, about 5 minutes; turn and cook the second side for 3 minutes. Return the chicken to the oven and bake until the juices run clear when a thigh is pricked in the deepest part and an instant-read thermometer reads 165°F., about 10 minutes.

Before serving, stir the pine nuts and chopped mint into the vegetable mixture. Serve the thighs over fettuccine, if desired, with a liberal amount of caponata on top. Garnish with the orange segments and mint sprigs.

HOMEY OVEN-ROASTED CHICKEN THIGHS AND LEGS WITH PAN GRAVY

This delectable chicken roasted in a deep or regular 10-inch cast-iron skillet is the epitome of easy comfort food. A cup of aromatic vegetables are browned along with the chicken and then puréed with some broth and lemon juice into the delicious home-style gravy. Serve with mashed potatoes for more old-fashioned goodness.

1 teaspoon kosher salt or sea salt

½ teaspoon dried thyme leaves

½ teaspoon freshly grated lemon zest, plus a few drops freshly squeezed lemon juice

⅛ teaspoon coarsely ground black pepper

Canola or other vegetable oil

2 legs-thigh combinations (about 1½ pounds), separated, excess fat and skin trimmed, and blotted dry

⅓ cup diced carrots

⅓ cup diced celery

⅓ cup diced onion

½ cup chicken broth

½ teaspoon Worcestershire sauce

Chopped flat-leaf parsley, to garnish

Preheat the oven to 350°F. In a small bowl, combine the salt, thyme, lemon zest, and pepper.

Heat a 10-inch cast-iron skillet over medium-high heat until hot but not smoking. Brush with a little oil, add the chicken, skin-side down, and cook until the skin is crisp and lightly browned and the pieces easily move in the pan, 6 to 7 minutes. Season with half of the salt mixture and scatter the vegetables in the pan.

Turn and cook the second sides until browned, about 3 minutes. Add remaining seasonings and transfer to the oven to roast until done and the juices run clear when the thigh is pricked deep in the flesh without touching the bone, about 30 minutes. Remove the pan from the oven, transfer the chicken to a plate, tent with foil, and keep warm in the oven.

On top of the stove, pour the chicken broth into the skillet, bring to a boil, and scrape up the brown bits from the bottom of the pan. Transfer to a mini food processor and purée until smooth. Add the Worcestershire sauce and lemon juice to taste and pulse to blend. Divide the chicken between two plates or leave on a platter. Serve with the gravy and garnish with a little parsley.

LAUREN'S CHICKEN BING

Bing sandwiches are a popular street food in China. They are made with a wide variety of fillings, including many that are vegetarian. My creative friend Lauren McGrath, a food project consultant and event producer, makes this easy, quick, and very satisfying version with chicken thighs, scallions, ginger, and Napa cabbage with purchased pizza dough from her local pizzeria.

She says the recipe is very flexible and you could make it with any number of fillings. For example, you could substitute pork shoulder or butt for the chicken, choose watercress instead of cabbage, and add some minced hot peppers, etc. Fresh pizza dough is also available at many markets.

4 ounces boneless skinless chicken thighs, coarsely chopped
2 scallions, white parts coarsely chopped, green parts finely chopped
½ tablespoon minced fresh ginger root
2 teaspoons soy sauce
¼ teaspoon kosher salt or sea salt
¼ teaspoon granulated sugar
⅛–¼ teaspoon ground Sichuan pepper or black pepper
1 teaspoon vegetable oil, plus oil to brush the pan
1 cup finely shredded Napa cabbage
8 ounces prepared pizza dough
Flour for rolling the dough
Chili garlic sauce (optional)

In a food processor, combine the chicken and the white parts of the scallions and pulse until the mixture is finely chopped. Do not over-pulse. Season with the ginger, soy sauce, salt, sugar, and pepper.

Preheat the oven to 450°F.

Heat a 9- to 10-inch cast-iron skillet over medium-high heat until hot but not smoking. Add the oil and chicken mixture and quickly stir-fry until just starting to brown, stirring often. Scrape into a bowl, and mix in the cabbage and scallion greens. Set aside while preparing the dough. Let the pan cool and wipe out with a paper towel.

Divide the dough in half. On a lightly floured board, roll the dough into two thin, flat rounds slightly smaller than the pan. It doesn't matter if the round doesn't reach to the very edges of the pan. Brush the pan lightly with oil.

Place one round in the pan and spoon the filling onto the dough, leaving about a ½-inch margin around the outside edge. Place the other piece of dough over the top, pressing down the edges onto the bottom piece to seal. Bake until browned, about 15 minutes. Using a wide spatula, transfer the bing to a rack to cool, 3 to 4 minutes, then cut in half, and serve with a little chili garlic sauce on the side, if desired.

TURKEY-FETA BURGERS WITH HARISSA AIOLI

Too often I find turkey burgers dry and boring. One good way to help keep them moist is to buy ground turkey that includes both light and dark meat. For taste, feta and lively Moroccan flavors along with cilantro are mixed in. Be sure to add enough oil so they don't stick to the pan and cook them over medium heat. The burgers are topped with a decadent aioli of mayonnaise, harissa, cucumbers, and shallot for a mouthful of scrumptiousness. Alternatively, use the Tahini-Yogurt Sauce from the Zesty Cauliflower, Pine Nuts, and Currants with Tahini-Yogurt Sauce on page 77.

HARISSA AIOLI
¼ cup mayonnaise
2 tablespoons finely chopped Persian or other cucumber
2 tablespoon minced shallot
2 teaspoons harissa
1 clove garlic, minced

TURKEY BURGERS
2 tablespoons minced cilantro leaves
2 tablespoons dried currants
½ teaspoon *ras el hanout*
¼ teaspoon kosher salt or sea salt
Freshly ground black pepper
¼ cup finely crumbled feta cheese
8–9 ounces ground turkey including dark meat
2–3 teaspoons canola or other vegetable oil, for the pan
2 brioche hamburger rolls or sliced whole grain bread
2 small romaine lettuce leaves
1 thinly sliced plum tomato

In a small bowl, stir the mayonnaise, cucumber, shallot, harissa, and garlic together until well blended. Set aside.

In a medium bowl, combine the cilantro, currants, *ras el hanout*, salt, black pepper, and feta. Add the turkey and gently mix to blend well. Form into two 1-inch-thick patties.

Heat a 10-inch cast-iron griddle, grill pan, or skillet over medium heat until hot but not smoking. Add the oil, lay the burgers in the pan, season with salt and pepper, and cook for 5 to 6 minutes, depending on the desired degree of doneness. Do not flatten with a spatula. Turn, season with salt and pepper, and cook the second side for about the same amount of time, adding the remaining oil if needed. Remove from the pan and let rest for a few minutes.

Spread some aioli on the top and bottom of the rolls or bread. Using a spatula, transfer the burgers to the bottoms, add a romaine leaf, some tomato slices, and another dollop of the aioli, and serve.

MOLE TURKEY POTPIE WITH CORN BREAD TOPPING

Turkey and mole are both Mexican natives and the two are traditionally combined for Christmas dinner. Rather than waiting for a special holiday, this flavorful potpie brings a fiesta of flavors whenever you crave an enticing comfort dish. The lively turkey is topped with corn bread. (If pressed for time, use a good-quality mix.)

In Oaxaca, I visited the much-loved and respected Susana Trilling, owner of Seasons of My Heart cooking school, and tasted my way through the city's seven famous mole sauces. To write about them, I contacted Phil Saviano, of VivaOaxacaFolkArt.com, who imports excellent Oaxacan moles and some delightful crafts into the United States. Having made mole a few of times from scratch, I suggest you find a reliable source for the authentic versions.

½ cup chicken broth
2 tablespoons prepared dark mole paste (I prefer VivaOaxacaFolkArt.com's Soledad)
2 tablespoons smooth or chunky almond butter
1 tablespoon canola or other vegetable oil
¼ cup finely chopped onion
1 large clove garlic, minced
7 ounces ground turkey with light and dark meat
½ cup diced red bell pepper
½ cup canned kidney beans, rinsed and drained
⅓ cup diced canned tomatoes with juice
2 tablespoons golden raisins
½ teaspoon kosher salt or sea salt
Freshly ground black pepper
2 tablespoons chopped cilantro leaves, plus a few leaves for garnish

In a small microwave-safe bowl, heat the broth and mole together in a microwave oven on high power until blended, about 2 minutes, stirring a few times. Or heat it in a small pan on the stove. Stir in the almond butter and set aside.

Preheat the oven to 375°F.

Heat an 8-inch cast-iron skillet over medium heat until hot but not smoking. Add the oil and onion and sauté until the onion is limp and golden, 2 to 3 minutes. Stir in the garlic, cook 30 seconds, add the turkey, and cook until almost no longer pink, about 3 minutes, breaking up the larger pieces with a wooden spatula.

Stir in the dissolved mole mixture. Add the red pepper, kidney beans, tomatoes, and raisins and season with about ½ teaspoon of salt, or to taste, and plenty of black pepper. Bring to a boil, stirring to blend. Simmer for a few minutes, then stir in the cilantro and keep warm while you prepare the

(Ingredients and Directions continued on next page)

CORN BREAD TOPPING

½ cup stoneground yellow
    cornmeal (I use Bob's Red Mill
    cornmeal)
¼ cup all-purpose flour
2 teaspoons granulated sugar
1½ teaspoons baking powder
¼ teaspoon salt
⅔ cup buttermilk
1 large egg, beaten
1 tablespoon melted unsalted
    butter or vegetable oil
Avocado slices drizzled with a
    little lime juice, to garnish

cornmeal mixture. The filling should be somewhat soupy.

In a medium-sized bowl, combine the cornmeal, flour, sugar, baking powder, and salt. In a small bowl, combine the buttermilk and egg; stir them into the dry ingredients until blended. Add the butter or oil and mix well. Using a large spoon or rubber spatula, spoon the batter over the meat, taking care to cover it well. Smooth the top with a slightly wet spatula or even your fingers.

Bake until the top is lightly browned, a toothpick inserted into the crust comes out clean, and the filling is bubbling up on the sides, 18 to 20 minutes. Remove the pan from the oven and let stand for at least 10 minutes. Garnish with avocado slices and a few cilantro leaves and serve.

CORNISH GAME HEN ALLA DIAVOLA

For centuries, Romans and Florentines have roasted chickens and other birds al mattone, or weighed down under a foil-wrapped brick to keep them flat and help them become crispy and juicy. When the bird's marinade includes red pepper, it's known as alla diavola, or devil's fare, for the peppery taste and charred flesh.

If you don't want to "spatchcock" the bird to remove the breastbone, cut out the backbone, as suggested below, then cut the breast side in half, remove the keel bone, and with a meat pounder or the side of a knife, pound the joints to flatten. Dry the hen well so the skin doesn't stick or tear when turning.

Besides a brick, a second cast-iron skillet works well as a weight on top of the bird so long as it doesn't completely cover the first pan (which would cause it to steam). Serve hot or at room temperature with Roasted Potatoes with Sage Leaves in Duck Fat (page 87) and a green salad.

1 Cornish game hen
  (about 1½– 2 pounds)
Leaves from 1 sprig rosemary, plus
  small sprigs for garnish
Leaves from 2 sprigs thyme
1 large clove garlic
½ tablespoon kosher salt or coarse
  sea salt
3 tablespoons extra-virgin olive oil
2 tablespoons freshly squeezed
  lemon juice, plus ½ lemon, cut
  in wedges, as garnish
½ teaspoon Tabasco sauce
  (optional)
1 brick, wrapped in heavy foil, or a
  second cast-iron skillet

Using kitchen shears, cut off the game hen's wing tips and trim off excess skin and fat. Remove the backbone by cutting along either side of the spine. Open the bird flat, turning it flesh-side down with the legs closest to you. Starting at the bottom point of the breastbone, run the tip of a knife along the bone, pulling up on the cartilage and bone to work it loose from the breasts, taking care not to tear the skin. Flip the rib cage back and chop off the bones. Make a small incision in the skin between the leg and thigh, partially separating the two sections. Make another small cut between the breast and wing sections.

Finely chop the rosemary, thyme, and garlic together with ½ tablespoon of salt. (You can do this in a clean coffee grinder, but don't make a paste.) Rub the mixture over the inside and outside of the hen and put it in a resealable plastic bag. Add the olive oil, lemon juice, and Tabasco sauce (if using); seal, squeezing

(Directions continued on next page)

out most of the air, and turn to coat evenly. Refrigerate for at least 4 hours or overnight, turning once or twice.

About an hour before cooking, remove the bag from the refrigerator to return to room temperature. Remove the hen from the marinade and pat dry with paper towels.

Heat a 10-inch cast-iron skillet over high heat until very hot but not smoking; lightly brush with oil. Lay the hen in the pan, skin-side down, and immediately place the foil-covered brick or second pan on top of the bird, pressing down to flatten it. Reduce the heat to medium and let the game hen cook undisturbed until the skin is richly browned and crisp, and the bird releases itself from the pan, about 15 minutes. Remove the brick or pan, turn the hen over, replace the weight, and cook until the juices run clear when pricked in the deepest part of the thigh, about 7 minutes, or when an instant-read thermometer inserted in the deepest part of the thigh reads 165°F.

Transfer to a warm platter, tent with foil, and let it stand for 10 to 15 minutes before cutting it in half, or into leg and breast portions, if desired. Serve garnished with lemon wedges and sprigs of rosemary.

CARIBBEAN CORNISH GAME HEN

For a tropical taste of the Caribbean, try this Cornish game hen simmered in coconut milk with tangerine and lime juices, mashed banana, ginger, red pepper flakes, and saffron. When blended, the sauce becomes mildly spicy (your call on the heat level). Serve over jasmine rice, if desired. A tall pineapple-rum-based drink or even hibiscus iced tea would be an appropriate beverage.

¾ cup full-fat coconut milk

Generous pinch saffron threads, crumbled

1 tablespoons canola or other vegetable oil, plus ½ tablespoon more, if needed

1 Cornish game hen, about 1½ pounds, split with backbone, wing tips, and excess fat removed, blotted dry

Kosher salt or coarse sea salt

Freshly ground black pepper

¾ cup finely chopped onions

Grated zest of 1 tangerine or 1 small orange, plus 2 tablespoons freshly squeezed juice

Grated zest of 1 lime, 1 tablespoon freshly squeezed juice or more, plus thin lime slices for garnish

1½ tablespoons minced fresh ginger root

1 small or ½ large very ripe banana, mashed

½ teaspoon ground nutmeg or mace (see page 153)

⅓ teaspoon red pepper flakes

2 tablespoons light rum

1 teaspoon turbinado sugar (optional)

Sliced coconut, toasted, for garnish (optional)

In a small microwave-safe bowl or small saucepan, heat the coconut milk until warm. Add the saffron and set aside.

Heat a 10-inch cast-iron skillet over medium-high heat until very hot but not smoking. Add the oil and game hen halves, skin-side down, to the pan. Reduce the heat to medium and cook until the skin is lightly browned and the pieces move easily, 4 to 5 minutes. Turn and cook the second side for 3 to 4 minutes. Season to taste with salt and pepper.

If the oil has burned, discard it, wipe out the pan, and add the remaining ½ tablespoon of oil. When hot, stir in the onions and sauté over medium heat until wilted and lightly colored, about 4 minutes, stirring often. Add the tangerine zest and juice, the lime zest, and the tablespoon of the lime juice, turn the heat to high, and boil until the liquid is reduced by half, about 1 minute.

Reduce the heat to medium-low. Stir in the coconut milk, ginger, banana, nutmeg or mace, red pepper flakes, and salt and pepper. Return the game hen to the pan, skin-side up, cover, and simmer until the chicken is cooked through, about 25 minutes, turning the pieces once or twice. Stir in the rum, the sugar if the banana wasn't ripe enough, and a little more lime juice, if desired. Garnish with a couple thin slices of lime and some toasted coconut on top, and serve.

Mace or Nutmeg: Two Siblings Separated

Both spices come from the nutmeg tree. When the bright red exterior webbing is removed, dried, and ground into a reddish powder, it is mace, a slightly stronger sibling of nutmeg. The pit is nutmeg. When ground, it is milder and a little sweeter.

PLUM-CHERRY GLAZED DUCK BREASTS

Duck never tasted more alluring than these succulent, aromatic glazed breasts brushed with plum-cherry preserves accented by a dash of soy sauce and a hint of Chinese five-spice seasoning. They're simple to make and you'll feel like a culinary pro. I first fell in love with magret de canard *while writing* D'Artagnan's Glorious Game Cookbook *with owner Ariane Daguin. Then I developed this recipe for my friends, Bill and Sarabeth Levine, at Sarabeth's Kitchen. For this dish, I also roast small Yukon Gold potatoes along with the duck as the fat melts into the pan. Or, you can strain the fat, save it in your refrigerator, and use it on another occasion for crunchy Roasted Potatoes with Sage Leaves in Duck Fat (page 87).*

1 (1-pound) *magret* duck breast (I buy D'Artagnan's)
Kosher salt or coarse sea salt
Freshly ground black pepper
4 ounces small Yukon Gold potatoes, quartered
¼ cup plum-cherry or other strained red fruit preserves
1 teaspoons soy sauce
¼ teaspoon Chinese five-spice seasoning
Sea salt
Freshly ground black pepper
Chopped cilantro leaves, to garnish

Trim excess fat from the breasts and carefully score the fat diagonally into small squares, taking care not to cut into the flesh. Pat dry and season generously with salt and pepper.

Heat a 10-inch cast-iron skillet over medium-high heat until hot but not smoking. Add the breasts, skin-side down, and the potatoes cut-sides down, and reduce the heat to medium-low. Slowly render the fat until only a thin, crisp layer of skin remains, about 20 minutes. Turn the potatoes occasionally to brown evenly. When the potatoes are done, transfer them to a small pan or skillet and keep warm.

While the duck cooks, preheat the oven to 400°F. In a small bowl, blend the preserves, soy sauce, and Chinese five-spice seasoning.

Turn the breast over and drain the fat from the pan. Season the duck with salt and pepper. Spoon 2 to 3 tablespoons of the preserve mixture evenly over the duck, transfer to the oven, and roast until rare to medium-rare, 7 to 8 minutes. Remove and let stand for 5 minutes. Thinly slice the breast across the grain and spoon any pan juices over the slices. Sprinkle on the cilantro and serve with the potatoes.

6. Meat

BLACK PEPPER-CRUSTED FILET MIGNON WITH CHIMICHURRI

To celebrate a big milestone or simply a good day, pepper-crusted filet mignon with chimichurri, Argentina's delectable garlicky green sauce, is a stellar main course. It's the epitome of simplicity, especially with an instant-read thermometer to ensure it's done to your taste. This is probably more chimichurri than you'll need, but use it on Leftover Steak and Manchego Quesadillas with Chimichurri (page 169) or on grilled chicken. I serve the filets with green beans or oven-roasted asparagus.

Black peppercorns are easily cracked in a resealable plastic bag with a meat pounder or the bottom of a heavy pan. You don't want them too fine.

FILET MIGNON

1 tablespoon coarsely crushed black peppercorns

1 teaspoon kosher salt or coarse sea salt

2 (6–7 ounces each) filet mignon about 1½ inches thick

CHIMICHURRI
(MAKES ABOUT 1 CUP)

1 cup packed cilantro leaves and parsley leaves

1 tablespoon fresh oregano leaves or 1 teaspoon dried

1 tablespoon chopped garlic

⅓ cup extra-virgin olive oil, plus ½ tablespoon for the pan

1 tablespoon red wine vinegar

⅛–¼ teaspoon crushed red pepper flakes

1 teaspoon freshly squeezed lime juice, or more to taste

Kosher salt or coarse sea salt

Freshly ground black pepper

In a flat dish, mix the peppercorns and salt together and firmly press both sides of the filets into the mixture. Set aside for the meat to come to room temperature, at least 20 minutes and up to 45 minutes.

In a food processor, combine the cilantro, parsley, oregano, and garlic and pulse until finely chopped. Scrape the mixture into a bowl, stir in the ⅓ cup of olive oil, vinegar, red pepper flakes, and lime juice; season to taste with salt and pepper. Refrigerate until needed.

Position a rack in the center of the oven and heat to 350°F. Meanwhile, heat a 10-inch cast-iron skillet or griddle over medium-high heat. Add the remaining ½ tablespoon of oil to the pan. When it is shimmering but not smoking, add the steaks and cook for 4 minutes without moving until nicely browned. Turn and cook the second side for 4 minutes. They will be quite rare (at or about 120°F). Transfer the pan to the oven and cook until an instant-read thermometer reads 120 to 125°F for rare; 130° to 135°F for medium-rare; 140 to 145°F for medium; total cooking time from 2 to 7 minutes more. Let stand 5 minutes.

Remove the chimichurri from the refrigerator and stir. Transfer the steaks to dinner plates, spoon on the sauce, and serve.

TUSCAN SHORT RIB RAGÙ OVER PASTA

One chilly night, I was craving a dish of succulent braised meat over pasta like I'd eaten in Florence, so I tweaked the bourbon-molasses version in my Cast-Iron Cookbook with some Italian ingredients like pancetta, fennel, capers, and rosemary. Along with the aromatics and tomatoes, the meat simmered in red wine and beef broth until it was fall-off-the-bone tender. We devoured two meaty short ribs apiece, but I felt I'd eaten too much.

To duplicate the comforting aspects of that meal with lots of rich sauce but less protein, I halved the short ribs but kept most of the sauce. When cooked, I shredded the meat, added it back to the ragù, then ladled it on pasta with Parmigiano-Reggiano sprinkled on top. It was a meal worth toasting with a robust Tuscan red wine. If you want more meat, double the short ribs while cooking, but use a larger pan.

¾ pound well-trimmed short ribs, cut into 2-inch pieces
All-purpose flour, for dredging
1 tablespoon extra-virgin olive oil, plus oil to drizzle on the cooked pasta
Kosher salt or coarse sea salt
Freshly ground black pepper
¼ cup (1 ounce) finely diced pancetta or thick sliced bacon
½ cup finely chopped fennel
1 small carrot, finely chopped (about ⅓ cup)
1 small rib of celery, finely chopped (about ⅓ cup)
1 small onion, finely chopped (about ⅓ cup)
½ tablespoon chopped garlic
⅓ cup robust Tuscan or other dry red wine

1 cup beef broth, divided
1 cup petite diced canned tomatoes, including juice, divided
1 tablespoon tomato paste
1 teaspoon small capers
1 bay leaf
1 piece orange zest, about 4 inches x ½ inch
1 small sprig fresh rosemary, plus small sprigs for garnish
1 teaspoon dried thyme
6 to 8 ounces dried rigatoni or other tubular pasta
Grated Parmigiano-Reggiano

(Directions continued on next page)

Heat an 8- or 10-inch skillet over medium-high heat until hot but not smoking. Meanwhile, dredge the short ribs in flour, patting to remove the extra. Add the olive oil to the pan and brown the short ribs on all sides, including the ends, about 7 minutes. Transfer to a plate. Season generously with salt and pepper to taste.

Add the pancetta to the pan, turn the heat to medium-low, and cook until the fat is rendered, 2 to 3 minutes, stirring once or twice. Stir in the fennel, carrot, celery, and onion and cook until wilted and lightly colored, about 5 minutes, stirring a couple times. Add the garlic and cook for 30 seconds more.

Pour in the wine, raise the heat to high, and bring to a boil. Cook for 2 minutes, stirring up any browned bits. Add half of the broth and half of the tomatoes, the tomato paste, capers, bay leaf, orange zest, rosemary, and thyme. Return the short ribs to the pan, cover with a lid or heavy foil, and simmer over low heat until completely tender, falling off the bone, and the bone slides out of the meat, about 2½ hours or longer, turning 4 or 5 times. After 1½ hours, add the remaining ½ cup of broth and tomatoes.

Remove the pan from the oven and discard the bay leaf and orange zest. Transfer the short ribs to a bowl until cool enough to handle, pull off and discard any gristle and fat, and discard the bone. Shred the meat and return it to the pan to simmer. If there is a lot of fat in the pan, or you want to serve the dish later, transfer it to a nonreactive pan, cover, and refrigerate until you can scrape the fat from the surface. Return it to the pan to reheat.

When ready to eat, boil the pasta in a pot of salted boiling water until al dente. Drain and stir in a little olive oil. Divide the pasta between two flat bowls, ladle the ragù over the pasta, sprinkle on Parmigiano-Reggiano to taste, add sprigs of rosemary, and serve.

SOUTHWESTERN LAMB SHANKS

Cranberries and chipotle chilies in adobo sauce impart a robust, tangy-sweet flavor to these succulent braised lamb shanks. Turning them a couple of times during cooking ensures they'll be uniformly fork-tender. Like most braised meats, the shanks improve with reheating, so you can make them up to three days in advance. If you do, transfer them to a nonreactive bowl, cover, and refrigerate them, then return them to the pan to slowly reheat.

½ tablespoon canola or other vegetable oil
2 lamb shanks, about 14–16 ounces each, blotted dry
Kosher salt
Freshly ground black pepper
½ cup chopped onion
1 clove garlic, minced
½ full-bodied red wine, such as Cabernet Sauvignon
1 cup fresh or frozen cranberries
½ cup beef broth
2–3 tablespoons honey
½ tablespoon minced chipotles in adobo, or more to taste
1 teaspoon ground cumin
2 tablespoons chopped cilantro, plus ½ tablespoon to garnish

Position the rack in the center of the oven and preheat to 325°F.

Heat a 10-inch cast-iron skillet over medium-high heat. Add the oil and when it shimmers, add the shanks and brown on all sides, 10 to 12 minutes, using tongs to turn. Remove to a bowl and season generously with salt and pepper.

If needed, add a little oil to the pan. Stir in the onion and sauté over medium heat until wilted and beginning to brown, 2 to 3 minutes, stirring with a wooden spoon. Add the garlic and cook for 30 seconds. Pour in the wine, stirring up any browned bits on the bottom of the pan, and bring the liquid to a boil. Stir in the cranberries, broth, 2 tablespoons of the honey, the chipotles, and cumin; cook until the berries begin to pop, about 5 minutes. Return the shanks to the pan, cover tightly with heavy foil or a domed lid, transfer to the oven, and cook until fork-tender, turning a few times, 2 to 2½ hours.

Transfer the shanks to a bowl and cover to keep warm. Return the pan to the top of the stove, skim any fat from the surface, and bring the liquid to a boil. Cook until it

(Directions continued on page 164)

lightly coats the back of a spoon, about 8 minutes. Stir in the 2 tablespoons of cilantro, season to taste with salt and pepper, and taste to adjust the flavors, adding the remaining honey and additional chipotle, if desired. Return the shanks to the pot, turning to warm them through, if needed. Serve sprinkled with the remaining cilantro on top.

If not serving right away, transfer the shanks and sauce to a nonreactive container to cool. Cover and refrigerate. Slowly reheat them in the cast-iron pan on top of the stove.

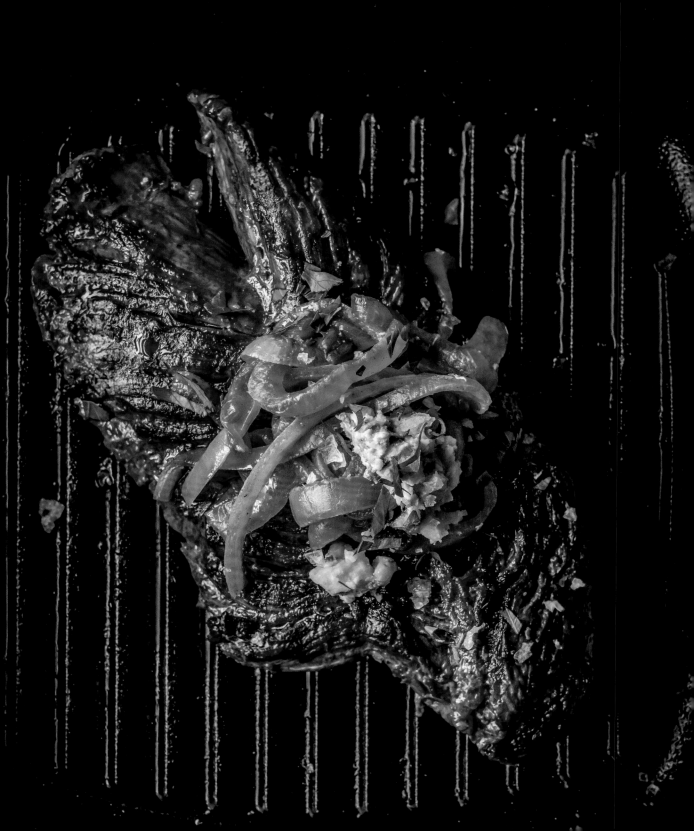

STEAK 'N' STOUT

This is one of my favorite go-to meals to share with a steak-loving friend. I prefer the meat crunchy on the outside and deep pink inside. While the steak sears in your grill pan or skillet, the stout–brown sugar marinade reduces over sautéed onions into a scrumptious, caramelized glaze. It's a heavenly combination. A knob of blue cheese, like creamy, semisoft Cashel blue from Ireland, makes it even more sublime. If you love hanger steak, perhaps buy somewhat larger pieces and use the remaining slices for Leftover Steak and Manchego Quesadillas with Chimichurri (page 169).

6 ounces stout or dark beer

2 tablespoons firmly packed dark brown sugar

1 tablespoon apple cider vinegar

1 clove garlic, split

1 bay leaf

1 to 1¼ pounds hanger, skirt, or flat iron steak

1½ tablespoons unsalted butter

1 teaspoon canola or other vegetable oil

2 very large yellow onions, thinly sliced

Salt and freshly ground black pepper to taste

2 ounces Cashel blue or other creamy blue cheese, softened

In a resealable plastic bag, combine the stout, brown sugar, vinegar, garlic, and bay leaf; add the steak and marinate for at least 30 minutes, turning once or twice. The meat may marinate for several hours.

In the meantime, in a large skillet, melt the butter and oil over medium-high heat. Add the onions and sauté until golden brown, 10 to 12 minutes, stirring often. (The first part of the onion preparation may be done ahead of time.)

Heat a 10-inch cast-iron grill pan over high heat for at least 5 minutes until very hot but not smoking. Remove the steak from the marinade, blot dry, and cook for 4 to 5 minutes on the first side. Turn and cook the second side for 3 to 4 minutes for medium-rare.

While the steak is cooking, remove the bay leaf from the marinade, and pour ½ cup of the marinade onto the onions, turn the heat to high, and boil until the liquid has mostly evaporated, stirring often, 6 to 8 minutes. Season with salt and pepper to taste and keep warm.

Once the steak is done, transfer it to a slicing board, season with salt and pepper to taste, and let rest for 5 to 10 minutes. Slice it across the grain and serve with the onions on top or as a bed under the meat slices. Add the blue cheese, if using, and serve.

LEFTOVER STEAK AND MANCHEGO QUESADILLAS WITH CHIMICHURRI

With leftover Chimichurri (see page 158), grilled steak or chicken, and shredded Manchego cheese, you can throw together this tasty quesadilla in no time. Want even more enticement? Add a dollop of bright-tasting, colorful pineapple-pepper-onion salsa on top. Or why not a spoonful of guacamole or Mexican crema to dress up your leftovers even more?

PINEAPPLE-PEPPER-ONION SALSA
⅓ cup finely diced pineapple
3 tablespoons finely diced red bell pepper
1½ tablespoon finely chopped red onion
1 small jalapeño, membranes and seeds
  removed, minced
1½ tablespoons freshly squeezed lime juice
2 teaspoons canola or other vegetable oil
1½ teaspoons agave nectar or to taste
⅓ cup chopped fresh cilantro leaves
⅛ teaspoon salt
Freshly ground pepper to taste

QUESADILLAS
Canola or other vegetable oil, to brush the pan
2 (9- or 10-inch) whole wheat tortillas
Canola or other vegetable oil, to brush pan
½ cup coarsely shredded Manchego cheese
4 ounces thinly sliced rare or medium-rare
  hanger steak, blotted with paper towels
3 tablespoons prepared or purchased
  Chimichurri (page 158)
Guacamole or Mexican crema, if desired, for
  garnish

In a bowl, combine the pineapple, red bell pepper, onion, and jalapeño. In a small bowl, whisk together the lime juice, oil, and agave nectar and pour over the salsa. Add the cilantro, salt and pepper, and toss again. Cover and refrigerate until needed.

Heat a 10-inch griddle or skillet over medium until hot but not smoking and lightly brush with oil. Lay one tortilla in the pan, sprinkle on half of the cheese, add the meat, and drizzle on the Chimichurri. Sprinkle on the remaining cheese, cover with the second tortilla, and cook until the underside is browned in spots, 3 to 4 minutes, pressing the top down with a spatula.

Turn and cook the second side until lightly colored and the cheese is melted, 2 to 3 minutes. Turn off the heat, cool slightly, and cut into six wedges with a sharp knife or pizza cutter. Add a spoonful of the Pineapple-Pepper-Onion Salsa to each wedge and serve with guacamole and/or crema, if desired.

HERB-CRUSTED RACK OF LAMB

Rack of lamb is the first choice of many carnivores for a special meal. It's also super easy to make. For two, buy a small rack of New Zealand lamb that weighs about a pound. They're sold "frenched," with the chine bone and fat between the ribs removed, and well trimmed. The mustard-herbed panko coating seals in the juices and keeps the meat juicy and delicious, so I serve it without a sauce. (If you'd like a sauce, béarnaise is a classic.) Be sure to remove the rack from the refrigerator about a half hour before cooking.

The meat should come out of the oven slightly undercooked, as the carry-over cooking time continues the roasting process for another 5 to 10 minutes. Serve with Lavender–Honey Roasted Butternut Squash (page 75) and/or Turkish Zucchini Pancakes with Yogurt-Cucumber Sauce (page 82).

3 tablespoons panko
1 tablespoons finely chopped flat-leaf parsley
2 teaspoons finely chopped fresh rosemary
1 clove garlic, minced
¼ teaspoon kosher salt or coarse sea salt
Freshly ground black pepper
1 tablespoon olive or vegetable oil, plus 1–2 tablespoons oil for the coating
1 rack of lamb (approximately 1 pound), frenched and all but a thin layer of fat removed
1¼ tablespoons Dijon mustard

Position the oven rack in the middle of the oven and preheat to 375°F. In a small bowl, combine the panko, parsley, rosemary, garlic, salt, and pepper to taste. (Or pulse in a mini processor to blend but do not overmix.) Heat a 10-inch cast-iron skillet over medium-high heat until very hot but not smoking. Brush with oil and place the rack in the pan, fat-side down. Using tongs, turn to brown all sides except the ends, about 7 minutes.

Turn the rack over, season with salt and pepper, brush the mustard over the meaty parts, and apply the panko mixture with a cupping motion of your hand, pressing to help it adhere. Drizzle a thin stream of oil over the crumbs, transfer the skillet to the oven, and roast until an instant-read thermometer inserted diagonally into the center of meat (but not touching the bones) reads 120°F, 15 to 17 minutes for medium-rare meat. For medium to medium-well, cook 5 to 10 minutes longer.

Remove from the oven, loosely tent with foil, and let stand for 10 minutes. The internal temperature will rise to 125 to 130°F for medium-rare. Slice into chops and serve.

MOROCCAN LAMB SHEPHERD'S PIE

For generations, shepherd's pies—a mix of chopped meat and vegetables with mashed potatoes on top—have been a staple in kitchens around the world. Many nationalities put their own imprint or flavorings on the homey dish. This version was inspired by my culinary adventures in Morocco, where their meat is often seasoned with an aromatic blend of sweet and savory ingredients and spices.

As we discussed for Moroccan Chicken Breasts with Cauliflower, Green Olives, and Pomegranate Seeds (page 131), ras el hanout, *their most famous spice blend, means "top of the shop," and refers to each spice vendor's favorite mixture, often with cardamom, coriander, cinnamon, cumin, chili flakes, ginger, smoked paprika, and turmeric. If you prefer, use ground beef or turkey rather than lamb. In Fez and Marrakech, I visited several spice shops. In the United States, it seems turmeric and smoked paprika are not as evident in many blends, so I added a little.*

YAM TOPPING

2 cups (about 10 ounces) yams or sweet
  potatoes, peeled and cut into 1-inch chunks
2 tablespoons milk
2 teaspoons unsalted butter or oil, plus oil to
  drizzle on the top
Kosher salt or coarse sea salt
4 tablespoons finely chopped cilantro leaves,
  divided, plus leaves for garnish

FILLING

1 teaspoon canola or other vegetable oil
6–7 ounces ground lamb
⅓ cup chopped onion
1 large clove garlic, finely chopped
2 teaspoons *ras el hanout*
¼ teaspoon smoked paprika
¼ teaspoon turmeric
⅓ cup diced canned tomatoes with juice
⅓ cup canned garbanzo beans, rinsed and
  drained
3 tablespoons dried currants
3 tablespoons slivered blanched almonds,
  toasted
Salt and freshly ground black pepper
3 tablespoons Greek yogurt mixed with cilantro
  leaves, for garnish, if desired

Fill a saucepan half full with salted water and bring to a boil. Add the yams and cook until tender when pieced with a knife, about 10 minutes. Drain well, add the milk and

(Directions continued on next page)

butter, and mash with a masher, fork, or handheld electric mixer until smooth. Season to taste with salt and stir in 1 tablespoon of cilantro.

Preheat the oven to 350°F.

Meanwhile, heat an 8-inch cast-iron skillet over medium heat until hot but not smoking. Add the oil, lamb, onion, and garlic and sauté until the meat is no long pink, separating the pieces with a wooden spatula, and the onion is wilted, about 3 minutes, stirring often. Stir in the *ras el hanout*, smoked paprika, and turmeric. Remove from the heat. Add the tomatoes, garbanzos, currants, almonds, and 3 tablespoons of cilantro. Season with salt and pepper to taste and stir to blend.

Spoon dollops of yam over the filling and smooth with a spatula to cover evenly. If desired, use the tines of a fork to make a decorative pattern. Transfer to the oven and bake until the filling is bubbling and the top is lightly browned, 20 to 30 minutes. If desired, drizzle a little butter on the yams and run under the broiler to brown in spots. Let stand for at least 10 minutes, sprinkle with chopped cilantro, and serve with a little yogurt-cilantro, if desired.

PORK TENDERLOIN WITH HONEY-BALSAMIC GLAZED PEACHES

Pork tenderloins are quick and easy to prepare. In this dressed-up version, the meat is seasoned with rosemary-sage salt and served with peaches glazed with chestnut honey and balsamic vinegar. The honey, from Italy, has a floral but slightly bitter back-of-the-palate taste that adds a sophisticated depth of flavor. If you can't find it, other floral or herb honeys can be substituted.

I first tasted the honey while working with Chef Michael White on his first cookbook. He made an ethereal pork roast with the delicate white peaches that are only fleetingly available in the United States. They are also quite fragile. Using flash frozen yellow peaches at the peak of their season may not be as glamorous, but they work wonderfully well here (and in the Peach-Rosemary-Ginger Crostata on page 204), and are available at almost any time of the year. Use a meat thermometer to be sure the pork is juicy and light pink in the center.

ROSEMARY-SAGE SALT
2 tablespoons kosher salt or coarse sea salt
1 tablespoon fresh rosemary leaves
1 tablespoon chopped fresh sage leaves
1½ teaspoons coarse ground black pepper
1 clove garlic
Grated zest ½ lemon
1 tablespoon olive oil
1 (1-pound) pork tenderloin, blotted dry

GLAZED PEACHES
1 tablespoon unsalted butter
1 cup frozen sliced peached, defrosted
1 tablespoon honey, preferably chestnut
2 teaspoons white or dark balsamic vinegar
1 small sprig fresh rosemary, plus small sprigs for garnish
¼ teaspoon Rosemary-Sage Salt (above) or to taste

In a clean coffee grinder or small food processor, combine the salt, rosemary, sage, black pepper, garlic, and lemon zest and process until fairly fine. (Any excess will keep for several days refrigerated or stored in a cool, dark place.)

Preheat the oven to 425°F.

Heat a 10-inch cast-iron skillet over medium-high heat until hot but not smoking. Add the oil and sear the tenderloin on all sides. Season liberally with the Rosemary-Sage Salt, transfer the pan to the oven, and roast until an instant-read thermometer reads 145°F, 14 to 15 minutes.

(Directions continued on page 176)

While the pork roasts, in a medium skillet or saucepan, melt the butter over medium-high heat. Add the peaches, cook for about 2 minutes, turning a couple times. Stir in the honey, vinegar, and fresh rosemary. Adjust the heat to medium-high and cook until the liquid glazes the peaches and they are tender, 3 to 4 minutes, stirring occasionally. Season to taste with Rosemary-Sage Salt and keep warm.

Once the pork is done, remove it from the oven and let it rest for 5 to 10 minutes. Cut across the grain into slices, spoon the peaches on top, and serve garnished with rosemary sprigs.

MERGUEZ, SHRIMP, EGGPLANT, AND PEPPERS

This colorful combination of North African lamb sausages, or merguez, *shrimp, eggplant, bell pepper, and onions recalls a wonderful holiday my kids and I spent in Andalusia, Spain, where the strong Moorish influence can be felt. The dish is seasoned with hot or mild smoked ground paprika (Pimentón de la Vera) with a final sprinkle of goat cheese for a tangy counterpoint to the rich flavors. If you have leftover cooked rice from another meal or even Chinese take out in your refrigerator, this is a great place to use about ½ cup of it. This dish is reminiscent of paella.*

2 tablespoons uncooked long grain white rice or
   ½ cup cooked rice
1–2 tablespoons olive oil, plus additional oil to
   drizzle on at the end
5 ounces *merguez* (lamb sausage) or spicy Italian
   turkey sausage, casings removed and cut in
   1-inch pieces
1 small eggplant, peeled and cut into ¾-inch
   cubes (about 2 cups)
1 small onion, diced
1 medium red bell pepper, seeds and
   membranes removed, diced
1 small rib celery, diced
1 large clove garlic, minced
6 ounces peeled and deveined large shrimp
1¼ tablespoons chopped flat-leaf parsley
Leaves from 2 sprigs fresh thyme or 1 teaspoon
   dried thyme leaves

2 teaspoons hot or mild Spanish smoked paprika
   (*Pimentón de la Vera*)
Salt and freshly ground black pepper to taste
¼ cup crumbled goat cheese
Julienned fresh mint leaves, to garnish

Preheat the oven to 350°F.

If you don't have leftover rice, fill a small saucepan with ¾ cup of salted water. Bring to a boil, add the rice, cover, and simmer over low heat until tender, about 20 minutes. Remove, let it stand for 5 minutes, or until any remaining water is absorbed; set aside.

(Directions continued on next page)

Heat an 8-inch cast-iron skillet oven medium-high heat until hot but not smoking. Add 1 tablespoon of olive oil and the sausage and cook until the pieces are no longer pink in the center, 3 to 4 minutes. Remove the pieces with a slotted spoon and set aside.

Add the eggplant, onion, bell pepper, celery, garlic, and remaining oil, if needed. Partially cover and cook until softened, about 7 minutes, stirring occasionally.

Stir in the shrimp, rice, parsley, thyme, smoked paprika, and salt and pepper to taste; cook until the shrimp just turn pink. Return the sausage to the skillet and stir to blend. Sprinkle on the cheese, drizzle with a little olive oil, and bake until the cheese and the filling are hot. Garnish with the mint and serve.

PAN-SEARED PORK CHOPS
WITH MUSHROOM RAGOUT

These pork chops seasoned with a Southern-style rub are flavorful and juicy. I prefer bone-in chops because they keep the meat moist and more flavorful. For even cooking and less shrinkage, remove the chops from the refrigerator about 30 minutes ahead of time and season them generously with salt at that time to allow the flavors to penetrate. Once seasoned, the pork takes minutes to cook. Because cast iron retains its heat, after the first side is seared, turn the heat down to low and use a thermometer to ensure the chops cook to 140°F of pale pink perfection.

I love them smothered with the Mushroom Ragout (page 183) or Beer-Glazed Onions (page 41), and served with polenta (see sidebar) or mashed potatoes. Any extra rub can be stored in a small covered jar in a cool, dark place. It's terrific for fried chicken or catfish.

½ tablespoon chili powder
1 teaspoon ground coriander
1 teaspoon ground cumin
1 teaspoon garlic powder
1 teaspoon salt
1 teaspoon firmly packed dark
   brown sugar
½ teaspoon ground black pepper
¼ teaspoon ground red pepper
⅛ teaspoon ground cinnamon
2 (¾-inch thick) center cut bone-in
   loin pork chops, blotted dry
Mushroom Ragout (page 183)
Stone-Ground Polenta (page 184)
1 teaspoon canola or olive oil
Kosher salt or sea salt
1 tablespoon chopped flat-leaf
   parsley, for garnish

In a small bowl, combine the chili powder, coriander, cumin, garlic powder, and a liberal amount of salt. Stir in the brown sugar, ground black and red peppers, and cinnamon. A half-hour before cooking, rub a teaspoon of the seasoning mix into each side of the pork chops.

Prepare the Mushroom Ragout, if serving; keep warm in an oven-safe bowl. Prepare the Stone-Ground Polenta, if desired, and keep warm over low heat.

Heat a 10-inch cast-iron skillet over medium-high heat until hot but not smoking. Brush with oil, add the chops, season with salt, reduce the heat to medium, and cook for about 4 minutes; turn, season the second side with salt, reduce the heat to low, and continue cooking until an instant-read thermometer reads 140°F when inserted into the thickest part of one of

(Directions continued on page 183)

the chops, close to but not touching the bone, about 3 to 4 minutes. Remove to a cutting board, tent with foil, and let rest for 5 minutes.

Spoon the polenta onto two dinner plates, add the chops, top with the mushrooms, sprinkle with parsley, and serve.

MUSHROOM RAGOUT

Mushrooms are so versatile and plentiful. I serve this robust mixture as a side dish or on top of grilled pork chops, as well as chicken or swordfish.

1 large clove garlic
1½ tablespoons chopped fresh oregano leaves
1 teaspoon salt
½ tablespoons extra-virgin olive oil
1 small yellow onion, thinly sliced
½ pound mixed mushrooms, like cremini, shiitake, and oyster, wiped, trimmed, and sliced
Pinch red pepper flakes
Freshly ground black pepper
½ tablespoon high-quality balsamic vinegar
½ tablespoon chopped flat-leaf parsley, to garnish

Preheat the oven to 400°F. Chop the garlic, oregano, and salt together until minced.

Heat a 10-inch cast-iron skillet over medium-high heat until hot but not smoking. Add 1 tablespoon of the oil and the onion and sauté until lightly browned, about 3 minutes, shaking the pan occasionally. Add the remaining oil, the mushrooms, oregano mixture, red pepper flakes, and a liberal amount of black pepper; cook for 1 minute, turning to coat the mushrooms with the seasonings and oil.

Transfer to the oven and roast until the mushrooms are golden brown and limp, about 12 minutes, stirring once or twice. Remove to the stovetop, stir in the balsamic vinegar, and cook for 1 minute over high heat; taste to adjust the seasonings, sprinkle on the parsley, and serve.

STONE-GROUND POLENTA

Slowly simmered, coarse-ground cornmeal produces an incomparably toothy yet creamy textured side dish with a satisfying taste. I've found cooking times can vary by different suppliers, so it's helpful to read the package directions. Stir the pot frequently with a silicone spatula, especially the bottom, and add salt at the end, if needed. Polenta is also an ideal partner for the Tuscan Short Rib Ragù over Pasta (page 161). If desired, stir in a couple tablespoons of grated Parmigiano-Reggiano or Pecorino Romano.

½ cup chicken broth
½ cup water or milk
½ teaspoon salt
⅓ cup stone-ground white or yellow cornmeal
1 tablespoon unsalted butter
Kosher salt or sea salt
Freshly ground black pepper

In a small saucepan, combine the broth, water or milk, and salt and bring a boil. Slowly whisk in the cornmeal until blended and smooth. Turn the heat down to low and simmer until the cornmeal is tender and the mixture has thickened, about 15 minutes or longer, stirring frequently with a silicone scraper to prevent the polenta from sticking to the bottom of the pan. If it gets thick and starts to dry out, stir in more water or broth, 2 tablespoons at a time, until smooth. Stir in the butter and season to taste with salt and pepper before serving.

BELGIAN PORK BRAISED IN CHERRY BEER

Throughout Belgium, many dishes are cooked with local beers, of which there are hundreds of varieties. This robust pork stew is simmered in kriek lambic, their famous cherry beer, along with mushrooms, pearl onions, and dried cherries. It's an inviting way to relax with a homey meal on a chilly evening.

I suggest using pork shoulder or pork butt, as the fat in these tougher, less expensive cuts of meat melts to add a delicious richness to the dish. A tablespoon of cream stirred in just before serving rounds out the tastes. Serve it over noodles, spaetzle, or frekkeh.

What to drink: the rest of the beer, of course. You can make the dish ahead, but transfer it to a nonreactive pan to chill if not eating it straight away.

10–12 ounces boneless pork shoulder or Boston butt, trimmed of large pieces of fat, cut into 1½-inch pieces, blotted dry
All-purpose flour, for dredging
2 tablespoons canola or other vegetable oil, divided
Kosher salt or coarse sea salt
Freshly ground black pepper
⅓ cup finely chopped carrot
⅓ cup finely chopped celery
⅓ cup finely chopped onion
1 clove garlic, minced
½ cup Belgian *kriek lambic* or American cherry beer

½ cup chicken broth
3 tablespoons finely chopped flat-leaf parsley, plus additional parsley to garnish
Leaves from 1 large sprig fresh thyme or 1 teaspoon dried
1 small bay leaf
6–8 pearl onions, or use frozen pearl onions
3 ounces small white mushrooms, wiped, trimmed, and sliced
3 tablespoons dried cherries or cranberries dried in cherry juice
1 tablespoon heavy cream (optional)
½ cup defrosted baby peas (optional)

Heat an 8- or 10-inch cast-iron skillet over medium-high heat until hot but not smoking. Dredge the pork in flour, patting to remove any excess. Add 1½ tablespoons of the oil and half of the pork to the pan and cook, turning regularly until richly browned on all sides, 6 to 8 minutes; remove to a bowl with a slotted spoon. Continue with the remaining pieces. Season generously with salt and pepper and set aside.

(Directions continued on page 186)

Add the remaining ½ tablespoon of oil, stir in the carrot, celery, and chopped onion, and sauté over medium heat until lightly colored, 4 to 5 minutes; add the garlic and cook 30 seconds. Pour in the beer and broth and bring the liquid to a boil over high heat, scraping up all the browned bits. Cook for 1 minute. Return the pork to the skillet. Add the parsley, thyme, and bay leaf; cover and simmer over medium-low heat until very tender, 75 minutes or longer, depending on the pork, stirring occasionally.

Meanwhile, if using fresh pearl onions, pare a thin slice from the root ends and cut a shallow "X" into them. In a small saucepan, liberally cover the onions with water, bring to a boil, and cook for 2 minutes. Drain, and when cool enough to handle, gently squeeze with your fingers to slip off the skins. Heat the remaining oil in a small skillet over medium-low heat. Add the pearl onions and sauté until lightly browned on all sides, about 6 to 8 minutes, shaking the pan often to cook evenly.

Uncover the pan, stir in the onions, mushrooms, and cherries, and simmer gently until the mushrooms and onions are soft, about 5 minutes. Remove the bay leaf, stir in the cream and peas, if using, taste to adjust the seasonings, and stir again. Serve garnished with a little parsley.

7. Desserts

APRICOT-COCONUT BREAD PUDDING

In the "happily using up leftovers" category: I made this custardy bread pudding with stale challah and the extra coconut milk in my refrigerator, along with chopped dried apricots, coconut flakes, and a splash of dark rum. In France, French toast is called pain perdu *(French for "lost" or "stale" bread). My Boozy Baileys Irish Cream French Toast made with stale brioche is on page 25.*

2 teaspoons unsalted butter, for the skillet
¾ cup full-fat coconut milk
2 tablespoons firmly packed light brown sugar
1 large egg
1 tablespoon dark rum
½ teaspoon pure vanilla extract
¼ teaspoon ground cinnamon
3–3½ cups loosely packed, stale challah or brioche, torn or cut into about 1-inch pieces
⅓ cup chopped dried apricots
¼ cup unsweetened coconut flakes
Confectioners' sugar, to sprinkle on top (optional)
Crème fraîche or lightly sweetened whipped cream, as topping

Preheat the oven to 350°F. Butter a 6-inch cast-iron skillet.

In a medium-sized bowl, whisk the coconut milk, sugar, egg, rum, vanilla, and cinnamon together. Add the bread cubes and turn to coat evenly. Soak until the liquid is almost absorbed, about 15 minutes. Fold in the apricots and coconut flakes.

Heat the skillet over medium-high heat. Scrape the bread mixture into the pan, transfer to the middle of the oven, and bake until a toothpick or knife tip inserted near the middle comes out clean, 30 to 35 minutes. Remove, let stand 5 minutes, lightly dust with confectioners' sugar, and serve with a dollop of crème fraîche or whipped cream, if desired.

BLACKBERRY-CANDIED GINGER CRISP

Fruit crisps and crumbles are the quintessence of home-style desserts. You can use any combination of fruits that please you—blueberries, of course, but also plums, peaches, etc.—and they're easy and fast to make. My current favorite is blackberries scented with a little candied ginger, topped with oatmeal-brown sugar streusel and vanilla ice cream or cinnamon-spiced whipped cream.

Unsalted butter to grease the pan

¼ cup granulated sugar or more, depending on the sweetness of the berries

1 tablespoon minced crystallized ginger

2 teaspoons cornstarch

½ tablespoon freshly squeezed lemon juice

2 cups blackberries

2 tablespoons chilled unsalted butter, cut into small cubes

⅓ cup uncooked oatmeal

¼ cup all-purpose flour

¼ cup firmly packed light brown sugar

¼ teaspoon ground cinnamon

Pinch salt

Vanilla ice cream or whipped cream sweetened with sugar and a little cinnamon, to garnish

Butter a 6-inch cast-iron skillet. Preheat to oven to 375°F.

In a bowl, combine the sugar, ginger, cornstarch, and lemon juice. Add the blackberries and gently turn to coat evenly. Scrape into the pan.

In a mini food processor, combine the butter, oatmeal, flour, light brown sugar, cinnamon, and salt; pulse until the mixture is the size of small peas; spoon over the berries. Transfer the skillet to the oven and bake until the fruit is hot and bubbling, about 25 minutes. Remove, let stand for 10 minutes, and serve with vanilla ice cream or cinnamon-scented whipped cream.

BLUEBERRY-LEMON CLAFOUTI

A clafouti is a custardy, fruit-filled pancake that is a classic French dessert. Most often they're made with cherries, but one of my newest favorites is blueberry with a citrusy hint of lemon. Some people like them with a fairly thick layer of custard, but I prefer them flatter with the berries just embedded and a slightly crunchy bottom from melted sugar. Serve it warm, straight from the pan either for brunch or dessert. It's easy and quick to make.

4 tablespoons granulated sugar, divided
3 tablespoons all-purpose flour
Pinch salt
⅓ cup whole milk
1 large egg
1 teaspoon pure lemon paste (I use Nielsen-Massey brand)
1 tablespoon unsalted butter
1 teaspoon light or dark rum
1 cup blueberries
Confectioners' sugar, to garnish
Sour cream or crème fraîche, to garnish

Place an 8-inch cast-iron skillet in the oven and preheat to 425°F. Let the pan heat for 10 to 15 minutes. In a medium-sized bowl, stir 3 tablespoons of the sugar, the flour, and salt together. In a separate bowl, beat the milk, egg, and lemon paste until blended; whisk them into the dry ingredients until completely smooth.

Carefully remove the skillet from the oven. Add the butter, swirl until melted, stir in the remaining sugar and rum, and boil briefly until melted. Add the blueberries and shake until coated and cover the bottom of the pan. Turn off the heat.

Pour the batter over the berries and transfer the skillet to the oven. Bake until the edges are richly browned, the pancake is slightly puffy, the berries are bubbling, and a knife inserted in the center comes out almost clean, 11 to 12 minutes. Remove and let stand for 10 minutes, dust with confectioners' sugar, and serve with a dollop of sour cream or crème fraîche.

DRIED CHERRY TARTE TATIN GLAZED WITH ORANGE MARMALADE

This delicious cherry tart with a hint of fresh thyme was created by my friend Peter McGrath, who grew up baking with his grandmother and definitely inherited her talent. The secret to the tatin's success, says Peter, is having enough liquid in the bottom of the pan for the fruit and, in this case, the sweet orange marmalade to form a glaze that remains runny enough to release easily when the tart is inverted onto a plate after baking.

The slightly crimped edges, gently pushed down the sides of the skillet, help contain the cherries by creating a small lip. As I mentioned in the recipe for Fontina, Dried Figs, Prosciutto, and Caramelized Onion Crostata (page 29), rather than measuring 6 tablespoons of flour for the dough, I find it quicker to use a ¼-cup and ⅛-cup measures.The dough can be made the night before.

6 tablespoons all-purpose flour (see above)

2 tablespoons very cold unsalted butter, cut into small cubes, plus 1 tablespoon for the cherries

Pinch sea salt

1+ tablespoon ice water, for the crust, plus ⅓ cup water for the cherries

½ cup dried sour cherries or cranberries dried in cherry juice

2 tablespoons sweet orange marmalade

⅛ teaspoon fresh thyme leaves, plus 2 small sprigs to garnish (optional)

1 tablespoon freshly squeezed lemon juice

1–2 teaspoons cassis (optional), to drizzle on top

Crème fraîche or lightly sweetened whipped cream for topping

In a mini food processor, combine the flour, 2 tablespoons of butter, and salt. Pulse a few times until the butter is the size of small peas. Drizzle on 1 tablespoon of cold water and pulse until the dough begins to pull together, slowly adding up to ½ teaspoon more, if needed. Gather the dough together and form into a small disk, dust lightly with flour, cover, and chill for at least 2 hours.

In a 6-inch cast-iron skillet, combine the cherries, ⅓ cup of water, the marmalade, thyme, and remaining butter. Bring to a boil and cook until the butter is melted. Remove from the heat, stir once or twice, stir in the lemon juice, and cool for 15 minutes.

Preheat the oven to 400°F.

Meanwhile, remove the dough from the refrigerator. On a lightly floured board, roll the pastry into a 6½-inch circle. Using the side of a small spatula or the side of your hand, press the edges toward the center, forming a small lip and reducing the circle to about 6¼ inches. Transfer to a plate and chill for 10 minutes.

Remove the dough from the refrigerator, lay it on the cherries with the thickened edge down, and gently work the edges slightly down the sides. Bake until the top is golden brown and the fruit is bubbling, about 25 minutes. Remove, run a small metal spatula around the edge, invert the pan onto a plate, and reposition any cherries that have fallen off and any glaze remaining in the pan. Add a couple small thyme sprigs in the center, for garnish, if using, and let cool for 10 to 15 minutes. If desired, serve with cassis drizzled over the tart and a dollop of crème fraîche or whipped cream.

FROZEN CRANBERRIES WITH HOT CARAMEL SAUCE AND RYE-ALMOND SPICE COOKIES: A FINNISH DESSERT

Some years back, I visited Finland six times from the dead of winter to midsummer's night. While exploring their culinary world with Anna-Meija Tanttu, then the dean of Finnish food writers, we visited TV food personality Kati Nappa. On a hot June afternoon, she served us frozen lingonberries with sinful hot caramel sauce drizzled over them. It was taste bud–tingling and delicious. Kati served them over tuiles or pancakes, but after writing about Finnish rye bread, I created rye-almond-cardamom cookies based on my great-grandmother's walnut cookies and, without fresh lingonberries, I used cranberries.

Rye-Almond Spice Cookies
(page 199)

CRANBERRIES
¼ cup firmly packed dark brown sugar
¼ cup heavy cream
1 teaspoon unsalted butter
1–1¼ cups frozen cranberries or lingonberries, not in syrup
Mint leaves, for garnish (optional)

Make the Rye-Almond-Spice Cookies.

In a 2-cup glass measuring cup or bowl, stir the sugar and cream together to blend. In a microwave, cook on high power until the sugar is melted and the sauce is slightly thickened, about 2½ minutes. Remove, stir in the butter, and let it stand while pulsing the berries in a food processor until coarsely chopped.

Divide the berries between small bowls, pour on the hot caramel sauce, add a cookie or two, and serve garnished with mint leaves, if desired. If the caramel thickens, warm it in the microwave for 10 to 15 seconds until pourable.

RYE-ALMOND SPICE COOKIES

2 tablespoons unsalted butter, at room temperature
2 tablespoons confectioners' sugar, sifted
⅛ teaspoon ground cardamom
⅛ teaspoon cinnamon
1 tablespoon unsweetened smooth almond butter
¼ cup rye flour
Pinch sea salt

Preheat the oven to 350°F.

In a medium-sized bowl, cream the butter, sugar, cardamom, and cinnamon until light and fluffy. Stir in the almond butter and mix well. Add the flour and salt to the first mixture and stir until smooth.

Lightly flour a workspace and pat the mixture into a 4-inch circle. Transfer to a 6-inch cast-iron skillet. Bake in the middle of the oven until the edges are golden brown, about 20 minutes. Remove the pan from the oven, cool in the pan, and cut into 4 pieces.

GORYBA: MOROCCAN ORANGE-SESAME SHORTBREAD

Makes 6 wedges

I adore shortbread and most cookies, but I rarely bake big batches except for special occasions. To satisfy my sweet cravings and have something to share when a friend comes for tea or a glass of sherry, I created this 6-inch skillet version of the orange-sesame shortbread cookies I first tasted at the home of Soumaya Cheb, a former restaurant chef in Fez, Morocco. Her husband Tariq was my guide to the medina, a World Heritage marketplace. When he found out I loved Moroccan food, he invited me to dinner with his family.

These delicate, not-too-sweet cookies were part of the lovely dinner Soumaya prepared. As a parting gift, she gave me a head scarf that I wore when I rode a camel into the Sahara desert at Merzouga (see page 132). The cookies are a cherished memory of this delightful shared experience and of how food connects us all.

⅜ cup (6 tablespoons or ¼ cup + ⅛ cup) all-purpose flour (see Small Kitchen tips)

2 tablespoons confectioners' sugar

¼ teaspoon baking powder

Pinch salt

3 tablespoons unsalted butter, chilled

½ tablespoon roasted hulled sesame seeds

½ teaspoon freshly grated orange zest, plus a little zest to sprinkle on the cookies before serving

In the bowl of a mini food processor, combine the flour, confectioners' sugar, baking powder, and salt and pulse to blend. Add the butter, sesame seeds, and orange zest and pulse into the size of fine meal. (Or, in a small bowl, cream the butter and sugar together until fluffy; add the dry ingredients, sesame seeds, and orange zest and mix well.) It will be crumbly.

Transfer to a 6-inch cast-iron skillet and, using your fingertips, press down until smooth. Prick all over with a fork and partially score into 6 pieces. Cover and refrigerate for about 30 minutes.

Preheat the oven to 300°F.

Bake the cookies in the middle of the oven until the edges are lightly browned, 25 to 30 minutes. Remove, prick, and score again, and cool in the pan. Sprinkle on the remaining orange zest, if using, and serve.

HAZELNUT-DRIED FIG UPSIDE DOWN CAKE

I grew up in Southern California, where Spanish monks first cultivated black Mission figs in America. I liked them well enough, but when Peter McGrath suggested a dried fig-hazelnut upside-down cake, I got excited. It evoked memories of Fig Newtons from my childhood, the delicious hazelnuts in Piedmont, Italy, and finally the all-American pineapple upside-down cake baked by Mita Antolini, a neighbor of my friend, Nancy Harmon Jenkins, the food writer, when I visited her in Tuscany. What a circuitous path to this sophisticated dessert. The delicious, not-too-sweet cake is more than enough for two, but I know you'll enjoy any leftovers for breakfast, lunch, or tea.

FIGS
11–12 dried mission figs, stemmed and cut in half lengthwise
Water to just cover the figs
1½ tablespoons firmly packed light brown sugar
1 tablespoon unsalted butter
2 teaspoons freshly squeezed lemon juice

BATTER
1 large egg, separated
1 tablespoon whole milk
¼ cup firmly packed light brown sugar
2 tablespoons melted unsalted butter
6 tablespoons (¼ cup + ⅛ teaspoon) hazelnut meal flour (I use Bob's Red Mill)
3 tablespoons all-purpose flour
1 teaspoon baking powder
Scant ¼ teaspoon salt
Sour cream or crème fraîche, for garnish

Preheat the oven to 350°F.

In a 6-inch cast-iron skillet, lay the figs cut-side down in the bottom the pan. Pour in enough water to just cover them. Add the brown sugar and butter and bring the water to a boil; cook until the sugar and butter are melted. Remove from the heat, stir in the lemon juice, reposition any figs that have moved, and set aside to cool while preparing the batter.

In a medium-sized bowl, stir together the egg yolk, milk, brown sugar, and melted butter until blended. In a separate bowl, stir together the hazelnut flour, all-purpose flour, baking powder, and salt; stir into the moist ingredients.

Whisk the egg white into soft peaks. Using a silicone spatula, start by folding a large dollop of egg white into the batter until blended. Continue adding dollops until the mixture is smooth. Using a large spoon, add the batter in dollops over the figs, smoothing to cover evenly. Bake in the middle of the oven until the top is golden and a knife inserted into the middle comes out clean, about 20 minutes. Remove, invert onto a cake rack, replace any figs left in the pan, and cool for at least 30 minutes. Serve with a dollop of sour cream or crème fraîche.

PEACH-ROSEMARY-GINGER CROSTATA

I love using herbs in unfamiliar, but ultimately exciting places, such as the rosemary that subtly scents the crust in this free form peach tart. A small amount of the herb is also added at the end. I've made it with peach preserves mixed with crystallized ginger or ginger preserves. Both versions are delicious. A final drizzle of bourbon adds an additional lift to the flavors. Using peaches picked and flash frozen at the height of the season brings the taste and texture of seasonal fruit conveniently to your freezer without the frequent disappointment of mealy, imported peaches. The Dried Cherry Tarte Tatin Glazed with Orange Marmalade (page 197) uses fresh thyme in the same way.

1 tablespoon granulated sugar

2 teaspoons minced fresh rosemary leaves, divided

½ cup, plus 3 tablespoons all-purpose flour

¼ teaspoon salt, plus a pinch

2½ tablespoons cold unsalted butter, cut into ½-inch pieces, plus butter to grease a griddle

1½ tablespoons ice water

5 ounces frozen sliced peaches cut in ½-inch thick slices (about 1 cup)

2 tablespoons peach or ginger preserves

½ tablespoon finely chopped crystallized ginger (omit if using ginger preserves)

1 teaspoon light or heavy cream

1 tablespoon coarse sugar

1 teaspoon bourbon (optional)

Crème fraîche or vanilla ice cream (optional)

In a mini food processor, pulse the sugar and 1 teaspoon of rosemary until finely chopped. Add the flour and ⅛-teaspoon salt; pulse again. Add the butter and pulse into the size of peas. Pour the water through the feed tube and pulse until the dough starts to come together. Turn it onto a lightly floured work surface, knead briefly, and pat into a disk. Cover with plastic wrap and refrigerate until chilled, about 30 minutes.

Meanwhile, in a small saucepan over low heat, warm the peach preserves until melted. Or gently heat them in a medium-sized glass bowl in the microwave. Stir in the ginger and remaining pinch of salt and cool slightly. Add the peaches, turning to coat evenly.

Remove the dough from the refrigerator. Butter a 10-inch cast-iron griddle or skillet.

On a lightly floured piece of parchment, roll the dough into a 10-inch circle, dusting with flour a few times and turning to roll it out evenly. Lift onto the griddle. Spoon the peaches and juices into the center, leaving a 1-inch border around the edges. Pleat the dough over the peaches and return it to the refrigerator for 30 minutes.

Preheat the oven to 425°F. Brush the dough with cream and sprinkle on the coarse sugar. Bake until the crust is crisp and golden and the juices are bubbling, about 25 minutes. Remove from the oven, drizzle the bourbon over the peaches, cool for 15 minutes, and sprinkle the remaining rosemary over the peaches. Serve warm or at room temperature with a dollop of crème fraîche or small scoop of ice cream.

OOEY-GOOEY COFFEE-TOFFEE CHOCOLATE BROWNIES

These decadent brownies are crisp on the top and ooey-gooey fudgy inside. For years, I sent a version of them as care packages to my kids at camp until the camp owners decided not to allow sweets. That's when several counselors asked for the recipe. While you can eat them warm, they're also delicious cool. Serve with ice cream or coffee scented whipped cream.

Note: A third cup of chocolate chips usually weighs about two ounces.

Butter to grease the pan, plus
   2 tablespoons unsalted butter,
   softened
¼ cup granulated sugar
2 ounces semi- or bittersweet
   chocolate, coarsely chopped,
   melted and cooled slightly, see
   Headnote
½ teaspoon coffee extract (I
   use Nielsen-Massey brand) *or*
   espresso powder dissolved in a
   little hot water
½ teaspoon pure vanilla extract
1 large egg
2 tablespoons all-purpose flour
⅓ teaspoon sea salt
2 (1.4-ounce) Heath bars or ½ cup
   toffee bits, pulsed into small
   pieces in a food processor

Preheat the oven to 350°F. Butter a 6-inch cast-iron skillet.

In a small bowl, cream the butter and sugar until light in color. Stir in the melted chocolate, coffee extract, vanilla, and egg.

In another bowl, combine the flour and salt, and toss with the toffee bits to coat. Add to the butter mixture and stir with a wooden spoon just until all the ingredients are mixed. Don't overmix. Scrape into the skillet and bake in the middle of the oven until a toothpick inserted in the center comes out almost clean, 20 to 22 minutes.

Remove the pan and let it stand for 15 to 20 minutes to eat warm with ice cream or whipped cream. You can also remove the brownies from the pan, wrap in foil, and refrigerate them in an airtight tin or resealable plastic bag.

CHIPOTLE-CINNAMON MOLTEN CHOCOLATE LAVA CAKE

In this "ta-da" dessert, as if by magic, within about 8 minutes, melted chocolate and butter stirred together with eggs, sugar, and flour emerge from the oven as Kathleen Kenny Sanderson's divine molten chocolate lava cake. I added a touch of chipotle chile powder and cinnamon along with Kahlúa-flavored whipped cream on top. A final sprinkle of Maldon Salt makes all the flavors sparkle.

You can make the batter up to two days ahead of time. Cover and refrigerate, then return it to room temperature before baking.

---

4 tablespoons unsalted butter, plus melted butter to brush in the pan
2 ounces high-quality bittersweet or semisweet chocolate, coarsely chopped
2 large eggs, plus 1 large egg yolk
3 tablespoons granulated sugar
1 tablespoon all-purpose flour
¼ teaspoon vanilla extract
¼ teaspoon ground chipotle chile powder (optional)
⅛ teaspoon ground cinnamon
⅛ teaspoon sea salt, plus flaked sea salt, like Maldon Salt, for final garnish
Whipped heavy cream beaten with a little sugar and Kahlúa

Preheat the oven to 400°F. Lightly brush a 6-inch cast-iron skillet with melted butter.

In a medium glass or other microwave-safe bowl, combine the butter and chocolate and microwave on high in 30-second intervals until melted and smooth, 30 seconds to 1½ minutes, stirring after each interval. Remove and set aside to cool.

In a bowl, beat the eggs and yolk with the sugar and flour until light and thick, about 1 minute. Stir in the vanilla, chipotle powder, if using, cinnamon, and ⅛ teaspoon salt. Scrape into the chocolate and stir to blend well.

Place the skillet on a small rimmed baking pan and bake in the middle of the oven until the cake has puffed up a bit, the top is barely set, but still jiggles slightly when shaken, 8 to 11 minutes (better under baked than over baked). Remove and let sit for 1 minute. Place on a heat-safe dish, sprinkle with a pinch of Maldon Salt, and serve topped with Kahlúa whipped cream and two spoons.

**Flavorful Black Bean Burgers
in Pita Pockets with Hummus and *Ajvar*,** page 56

Appendices

Cooking With Cast Iron

In the beginning

When you get your first cast-iron pan, like countless new owners, you'll probably want to run to the kitchen and start cooking some of those soul-satisfying and delicious dishes you remember from childhood, tasted at friends' houses, read about in magazines, or watched chefs on TV and in restaurants prepare.

You take it out of the box or unwrap it and (hopefully) read whatever directions are included . . . and then you ask: *What do I do now? Do I need to season my pan even if it's supposedly "preseasoned"? If food sticks during cooking, how can I get it off, especially since I thought they were supposed to be nonstick? What if I accidentally leave my skillet in water and it rusts?*

Rest assured, you'll discover that cooking with cast iron has a quick learning curve, especially if you use it again and again and again. The more you cook, the better seasoned the pan will become, and the more comfortable you'll become with cooking virtually everything in this cookware.

What exactly is *seasoning,* you ask? Cast-iron pans are seasoned to develop the rich black patina that makes them nonstick. It doesn't happen overnight, and it's a somewhat imprecise process. During the cooking process, all foods release fat onto the cookware. With all new cast-iron pans, even "preseasoned" ones, you want to start building up a layer from the residue from the carbon molecules in oils and fats by repeatedly cooking foods—especially fatty foods to begin with—then wiping them clean. By heating and cooling down the molecules on the surface, they gradually meld together and develop what is called a hard, polymerized finish that eventually becomes shiny, black, and nonstick.

Hopefully, the following guidelines show you that cast-iron pans are easy to care for and use with cooking techniques from searing and sautéing, to broiling and baking, plus stewing and deep-frying.

- Wash a new cast-iron pan with warm water (mild dish detergent may be used, if so desired), and dry very well. Rub a light amount of the oil or fat of your choice all over it. After cooking, allow the pan to completely cool.
- The first few times you use a pan, including a preseasoned one, cooking fatty foods in it will speed up the seasoning process and help build up the

polymerized surface. Wait until after you've prepared several dishes in the pan before cooking eggs, omelets, and delicate fish to ensure success.

- Before adding fat to the pan when cooking, heat it for 3½ to 4 minutes over medium to high heat until hot but not smoking, unless otherwise indicated in the recipe. To heat a skillet or grill pan to where the heat is evenly distributed to sear meat like Black Pepper–Crusted Filet Mignon (page 158) or create the hash marks on Grilled Belgian Endive with Anchovy Vinaigrette (page 85), place the pan in a hot oven for 20 to 25 minutes.
- For a pan in which strong-smelling foods have been cooked, wash (with dish detergent, if you wish), dry, and then brush with a little oil and put it in a hot oven for about 10 minutes to diminish any residual tastes that might be imparted to other foods cooked in the pan.

Cooking with Cast Iron on Induction and Electric Cooktops

- It's worth noting that the surface of an uncoated cast-iron pan is somewhat rough, so it can scratch a glass top. For that reason, be careful about sliding the pans across the top.
- Unlike a gas stove, where the flame is directly under the pan, a cast-iron pan on an electric cooktop will take a little longer to heat up. Lodge, the country's oldest cast-iron company still in existence, suggests heating cast-iron pans on low and slowly raising the heat to medium or medium-high to get the most even heat throughout the pans.

A Word about Cooking with Acidic Ingredients

- When I first learned to cook with cast-iron, I was told *never* to cook with tomatoes, wine/vinegar, and citrus juices. After decades of testing this in all kinds of recipes, I say if your pan is well seasoned and you don't let acidic ingredients simmer for over 30 minutes, you should be fine. The worst that will happen if it stays much longer is you may get a subtle metallic taste.
- You can also avoid this when cooking with wine or citrus, as in Poached Arctic Char Provençal with Fennel Vinaigrette (page 111), by diluting the wine with water to reduce the acid. Or by adding it later in the cooking process. More important, once a dish like Braised Tuscan Short Rib Ragù over Pasta (page 167) is done, transfer it to a container to cool and skim off the fat, if needed, then cover tightly, and refrigerate when eating several hours later or a day or two after. Reheat in the pan when ready to serve.

Cleaning Cast Iron

With thanks to my friends at Lodge Cast Iron. (lodgemfg.com)

If you just bought a new cast-iron skillet that's maybe preseasoned, resurrected your mom or grandmother's Dutch oven that seems to be in decent shape, or found a pan at a yard sale with some rust and other gunk on it, you're probably wondering what do you do to create the black pan magic that so many people talk about.

As you've probably heard many times lately, with proper care, cast-iron cookware requires very little maintenance and can last for decades, if not centuries, so you can pass on a favorite pan to your kids and grandkids. It's the proper care part we want to focus on here: If needed, getting it back into a serviceable state and then using it often to keep it at its best.

Starting with the simplest issue: If there is residue on the cookware that is difficult to remove, use a silicone scraper to remove it. If the residue persists, make a paste of coarse salt and water and rub it into the surface to remove it, then rinse. For more difficult residue, put water in the cookware and bring to a boil and the residue will release itself from the cookware.

Under no circumstances should you leave water in your pan for an extended period of time or overnight.

Do not put cast-iron pans in a dishwasher. They wash away the seasoning and the pans often rust. Generally, I wash my pans, dry them well, and set them upside down over medium heat to remove any remaining moisture. Next, I apply a fine coating of oil or shortening. It should just wet the surface and shouldn't run. Wipe off enough of the heated oil to leave the pan with a dull shine. As you use the piece and continue with this maintenance seasoning process, your pan will develop a nice black patina and a nonstick surface.

To remove a small amount of rust: Rub the affected area(s) with steel wool. Rinse with warm water and a nylon scrub brush. Rub a light amount of the oil or fat of your choice on the rusted area.

To clean cast iron that's dirty, crusted with burned-on food residue, and maybe slightly rusted: If you find a neglected pan at your mom's house or at a yard sale, you can often restore it by following these steps.

- Place aluminum foil on the bottom rack of your stove. Place the cookware upside down on the middle rack. Close the oven door, lock if necessary, and set to self-cleaning. This takes about four hours in most ovens and will burn off all of the seasoning and crusted and burned-on food. Placing the cookware upside down allows the residue to fall to the aluminum foil. (Or, if you have an outdoor grill, place the cookware on the bottom of the grill. Place charcoal all over the cookware and light the charcoal.)
- Once the self-cleaning cycle is complete, or the charcoal is completely burned, allow the cookware to cool. Rinse with warm water and a nylon scrubby brush. Follow the seasoning instructions.

To salvage completely rusted cast-iron cookware: Place aluminum foil on the bottom rack of your oven. Preheat the oven to 350°F. Rub steel wool all over the cookware. Rinse with warm water and a nylon scrub brush and dry well. Rub a light amount of the oil or fat of your choice all over the cookware. Place the cookware on the middle rack of your oven and "bake" for an hour. After an hour, turn the oven off and let the cookware cool in the oven. If the seasoning isn't to your desired level, season again or cook something with a high fat content in the pan.

Cookware for Two

Cooking for two with cast iron doesn't require a lot of special equipment or pans. Most every recipe in this book was made in my 6-, 8-, or 10-inch skillet. A new favorite pan is a 10-inch griddle for making pizzas, pancakes, grilled cheese sandwiches, etc. I also love a grill pan for cooking steaks or searing vegetables when I want hash marks.

For other tools, you already probably own most of what's on the list that follows— and those are just personal suggestions— but we all know the right tools can make cooking easier and more enjoyable.

- 1-, 2-, and 4- cup glass measuring cups plus metal measuring cups, including ⅛-cup)
- 12-inch ruler
- 8-inch chef's knife and 4-inch paring knife
- Box grater
- Colander
- Deep-fat thermometer for frying
- Electric blender with 700 watts of power
- Good vegetable peeler and can opener
- Good-quality protective potholders and mitts
- Instant-read meat thermometer
- Measuring spoons, including ⅛ teaspoon and ½ tablespoon
- Microplane for zesting
- Mini- and/or regular-sized food processors, including one with a slicing blade
- OXO handheld mandoline slicer
- Pepper mill and/or coffee grinder to pulverize spices
- Plastic scrapers and a soft bristle dish brush for cleaning pans with stuck-on food
- Silicone scrapers, wooden spoons, wooden spatulas, and a slotted spoon
- Small- and medium-sized stable cutting boards
- Small- and medium-sized stainless-steel strainers
- Small metal spatula or spreader (Berndes' nonstick heat-resistant plastic spatula is inexpensive and very useful)
- Small- or medium-sized stainless-steel sauté pans

- Small-sized baking sheet to help maneuver a full skillet and prevent oven spills
- Splatter guard for frying
- Stainless steel kitchen tongs with silicone tips (10- and/or 12-inch sizes)
- Trivet for hot pans

A few words about a mini food processor: As someone who routinely used a big food processor for decades, and not a cook who buys every new piece of equipment that comes on the market, I was surprised and pleased at how useful Cuisinart's Mini-Prep Plus processor has been for making crusts and cookies in an appropriate size for two. I also use it for puréeing, chopping, making sauces, salad dressings, etc. There are other brands on the market many of which are also very good, but having a manageable size processor really helped. That said, there are still times when you also need an electric blender.

Shopping for Two

Countless ingredients, from the mundane to the obscure, can be purchased online from vendors around the world and across town. It's such an amazing convenience. When cooking for two, however, the challenge is that the sizes, quantities, and minimum orders are often fairly large. You need to weigh the convenience versus the cost.

At your regular grocery store, how much do you need to buy as an intelligent shopper? Even when the price is low, some bargains aren't really a bargain, especially if you throw most of the product away because it's dried or moldy, or takes up a lot of your premium shelf space. Here are some of my strategies for shopping for two:

Salad Bars

Salad bars have been around for decades but take a fresh look at how these expansive displays of produce, olives, pickles, legumes, tofu, etc. can work for you. Obviously, first check out that the area is well tended and clean, with a fast turnover.

If you're buying only torn lettuce or shredded carrots, then $6.99 or $7.59 a pound is pricey, and you might find those same ingredients sold with other produce items. But, by adding small amounts of olives and sun-dried tomatoes to a North African

Sausage Pizza in Phyllo (page 48), or a handful of nuts to garnish that you'd otherwise have to buy in jars or packages, and might not use in the near future, then you're benefitting from both the convenience of already cut or shredded ingredients and the savings realized from buying smaller portions.

Precut Vegetables and Fruits

If you can use up a bunch of fresh carrots or celery quickly, fine. If not, buy containers of cut up vegetables, such as carrots, celery, and onions (the aromatic base for stews), or broccoli florets and butternut squash—but, again, only if you will use them in the near future. Once cut, vegetables and fruits tend to deteriorate quickly. Grocers are also stocking more small-sized packages of broth and canned beans, for example, and even kid-sized boxes of raisins.

For making the Peach-Rosemary-Ginger Crostata (page 204), most of the year I buy flash-frozen sliced peaches that far excel those that are sold out of season, and the prices are better, especially when the peaches are used in cooking or baking.

Bulk Foods Bins

These can also be economical if you need a small amount of an ingredient that you wouldn't use often, such as dried figs for the Hazelnut-Dried Fig Tart on page 202. (I bought about 3 ounces for about $1.47, while a 12-ounce container at a local market was $13.99.) I also recycle empty glass spice and oil containers, refilling them when I buy smaller quantities of loose spices or dried fruits, or I share a large container with a friend.

Pre-Blended Ethnic Seasonings

These are now found in small jars and packages in many markets. Sometimes they are of value but not always. For example, buying a jar of *ras el hanout* saves you the time of buying and blending upwards of a dozen spices, but pumpkin pie spice mix includes only five seasonings that you might already have on your shelf, so that one specialty jar can be fairly expensive. Also check out ethnic markets where local seasonings are often very reasonably priced.

Spices, Pastes, and Herbs

Tubes of herbs and pastes are a newer convenience item that prolongs the usefulness of seasonings. Tomato paste and harissa have been available in tubes for years. More recently, Gourmet Garden's line of 8-ounce stir-in pastes come in all-natural tubes of basil, lemongrass, cilantro, even garlic and chunky garlic. A little dab can be a quick fix to brighten many a dish.

Unless I am testing large-quantity recipes, I rarely use up a full bunch of basil before it wilts, but I crave that flavor. My solutions are the Quick Homemade Pesto (page 12) and Basil Oil (page 63).

Finally, I enjoy fresh thyme both in desserts like the Dried Cherry Tarte Tatin Glazed with Orange Marmalade (page 197), and in numerous savory recipes. But the tiny fresh leaves dry out quickly, so when they do, I rub the sprigs between my palms over a bowl to release them and store them in a small herb jar, so I never seem to need to buy thyme.

A Few More Small-Sized Thoughts

- If making a bread pudding, consider buying Italian sub rolls, kaiser rolls, or a mini brioche if you won't eat the rest of a larger loaf.
- In many recipes, **shallots** can be a useful stand-in for small onions. I generally figure that a small onion is ⅓ to ½ cup sliced or diced.
- **Persian cucumbers** are not only a practical size when cooking for two, they have fewer seeds and a more intense flavor. They are among my favorite newer items now turning up in most markets.
- **Japanese or Italian eggplants** are a smaller, more user-friendly size than larger American globe eggplants. There are also small zucchini, etc.
- And, **miniature liqueur bottles** are ideal for spirits that you use as flavorings but don't usually drink, like Baileys Irish Cream, dark rum, Sambuca, etc.

Thank-Yous

Writing a cookbook can be a joyful and rewarding process. It's also a lot of work and, as many authors discover, almost impossible to accomplish alone. I feel blessed that many friends and colleagues generously contributed their time, professional skills, and encouragement to help bring this book to fruition.

To Deri Reid and Joan Brunskill, my editorial superstars and good friends, sincerest gratitude for your invaluable input that lent clarity to my words. Mark Kelly, thank you for sharing your professional knowledge in all things cast-iron, your wit, and for writing the foreword. Add to this, gifted writers/friends Nancy Harmon Jenkins, Emily Rubin, Suzanne Gerber, and Meryle Evans for reading and re-reading different versions of this book, always with enthusiasm and helpful suggestions. At Skyhorse, sincerest thanks to Nicole Frail for shepherding this book through.

Many friends did double- and triple-duty: talented chefs and professional cooks Lauren and Peter McGrath, Kathleen Kenny Sanderson, Renée Marton, and May Fridel, I'm so pleased you shared your recipes, tested others, and offered helpful suggestions. Also, to those who willingly chopped, dice, prepped, and cleanedup: Sebastiano Tronchetti, Deri Reed, Lauren McGrath, Lynn Bernstein, thanks for making this a team effort.

Noah Fecks, your unique talent coupled with patience, good humor, and a willingness to work like a demon created exciting, tempting pictures. It's miraculous how they all got done and I'm very grateful.

Many friends also shared their housewares and accessories to visually frame the dishes: Ilze Thielmann and Aitken Thompson, Marilee Hovet, Céline Kingsley and Mark Levy, Jani Jussel Brown, Rory Hayden, Maria "Bing" Reid, and Liza Schoenfein. Nan Whitney, as always, your keen photographic sense of my food in pictures is appreciated, as is the last-minute help from Oleg Logovskoy, Jr.

For the willing tasters and testers: Sarah Comerford, Michele Kelber, Mary Kirkpatrick, Barbara Koplin, Andrzej and Majka Krakowski, Gudrun Lange, Bruce Robertson and Lynne Van Auken, Emily Rubin, and Kelsey Brow, you helped make the experience more joyful.

Many thanks to David Leite, of LeitesCulinaria.com, for his great support.

To all of you (and anyone I may have forgotten), I am profoundly grateful.

Special thanks also go to:

Mark Kelly, Lodge Cast Iron Company

Ariane Daguin, D'Artagnan

Judi Arnold, Dufour Pastry Kitchens

Craig, Beth, and Matt Nielsen, Nielsen-Massey Fine Vanillas & Flavors.

Bill and Sarabeth Levine, Sarabeth's Kitchen

Elyse and Michael Harney, Harney & Sons Fine Teas

Nick Ciotti, Vanns Spices

Franklin Carrasco, produce manager at my Upper Westside NY Associated Supermarket

Tanairi Sanchez, front end supervisor, Upper Westside NY Fairway Market

Danny Vargas, fishmonger, Upper Westside Fairway Market

About the Author

Joanna Pruess is an award-winning food and travel writer who has written extensively about food for the *New York Times Magazine*, the *Washington Post*, the Associated Press, *Fine Cooking*, and PBS' online magazine: NextAvenue.org. She lectured about food and cultural anthropology at the Smithsonian Museum in Washington, D.C., The New School and the Morris-Jumel Mansion, in New York City, onboard the Crystal Cruises, throughout the United States, and in Istanbul and Izmir, Turkey.

Her fourteen previous cookbooks include *Soup for Two: Small-Batch Recipes for One, Two, or a Few; The Tea Cookbook; The Cast-Iron Cookbook*; and *Seduced by Bacon: Recipes and Lore about America's Favorite Indulgence*. Pruess was a regular contributor to *Specialty Foods Magazine* where she developed recipes for gourmet retailers and fine markets across the country and wrote about global cuisines.

In Parma, visiting Barilla Pasta and hearing "Rigoletto."

Joanna Pruess created and was the first director of the Cookingstudio, a cooking school within Kings Super Market, in New Jersey, where she and her thirty teachers had about fifteen thousand students in five years. Among the unique classes she taught were those specifically for vision-and hearing-impaired students and those with learning disabilities. She also taught in underserved schools and the prison system. She was honored by NYU's School of Foodservice as the Woman of the Year in Foodservice, Merchandising and Promotion. She resides in New York City.

Signing books at Google in London after serving three recipes in their dining room.

I have known **Chef José Andrés** since the early 1990s and long admired his passionate dedication to his community. In 2010, his sights became global when he started World Central Kitchen to organize prepared food in Haiti following their devastating earthquake. In so doing, he launched a new kind of hunger relief, a tsunami (or huge wave) of volunteers, who tirelessly cook and serve food in places where disaster has struck, including the Dominican Republic, Nicaragua, Cambodia, and even Washington, DC during the government shutdown. Andrés believes food can become an agent of change after disasters: building kitchens that improve health, increasing education rates, providing career skills, and creating food businesses.

For all of World Central Kitchen's positive efforts, I have chosen to donate a percent of my profits from *Cast-Iron Cooking for Two* to this extraordinary organization.

Index

Conversion Charts

Metric and Imperial Conversions

(These conversions are rounded for convenience)

Ingredient	Cups/Tablespoons/ Teaspoons	Ounces	Grams/Milliliters
Butter	1 cup/ 16 tablespoons/ 2 sticks	8 ounces	230 grams
Cheese, shredded	1 cup	4 ounces	110 grams
Cream cheese	1 tablespoon	0.5 ounce	14.5 grams
Cornstarch	1 tablespoon	0.3 ounce	8 grams
Flour, all-purpose	1 cup/1 tablespoon	4.5 ounces/0.3 ounce	125 grams/8 grams
Flour, whole wheat	1 cup	4 ounces	120 grams
Fruit, dried	1 cup	4 ounces	120 grams
Fruits or veggies, chopped	1 cup	5 to 7 ounces	145 to 200 grams
Fruits or veggies, pureed	1 cup	8.5 ounces	245 grams
Honey, maple syrup, or corn syrup	1 tablespoon	0.75 ounce	20 grams
Liquids: cream, milk, water, or juice	1 cup	8 fluid ounces	240 milliliters
Oats	1 cup	5.5 ounces	150 grams
Salt	1 teaspoon	0.2 ounce	6 grams
Spices: cinnamon, cloves, ginger, or nutmeg (ground)	1 teaspoon	0.2 ounce	5 milliliters
Sugar, brown, firmly packed	1 cup	7 ounces	200 grams
Sugar, white	1 cup/1 tablespoon	7 ounces/0.5 ounce	200 grams/12.5 grams
Vanilla extract	1 teaspoon	0.2 ounce	4 grams

Oven Temperatures

Fahrenheit	Celsius	Gas Mark
225°	110°	¼
250°	120°	½
275°	140°	1
300°	150°	2
325°	160°	3
350°	180°	4
375°	190°	5
400°	200°	6
425°	220°	7
450°	230°	8